Understanding and Facilit Organizational Change in the 21st Century

Recent Research and Conceptualizations

Adrianna J. Kezar

ASHE-ERIC Higher Education Report Volume 28, Number 4
Adrianna J. Kezar, Series Editor

Prepared and published by

 **JOSSEY-BASS**
A Wiley Company
San Francisco

In cooperation with

ERIC Clearinghouse on Higher Education
The George Washington University
URL: *www.eriche.org*

Association for the Study
of Higher Education
URL: *www.tiger.coe.missouri.edu/~ashe*

WASHINGTON DC

Graduate School of Education and Human Development
The George Washington University
URL: *www.gwu.edu*

Understanding and Facilitating Organizational Change in the 21st Century:
Recent Research and Conceptualizations
Adrianna J. Kezar
ASHE-ERIC Higher Education Report Volume 28, Number 4
Adrianna J. Kezar, Series Editor

This publication was prepared partially with funding from the Office of
Educational Research and Improvement, U.S. Department of Education, under
contract no. ED-99-00-0036. The opinions expressed in this report do not
necessarily reflect the positions or policies of OERI or the Department.

ISSN 0884-0040   ISBN 0-7879-5837-9

The ASHE-ERIC Higher Education Report is part of the Jossey-Bass Higher
and Adult Education Series and is published six times a year by Jossey-Bass,
989 Market Street, San Francisco, California 94103-1741.

For subscription information, see the Back Issue/Subscription Order Form in the
back of this journal.

Prospective authors are strongly encouraged to contact Adrianna Kezar, Director,
ERIC Clearinghouse on Higher Education, at (202) 296-2597 ext. 214 or
akezar@eric-he-edu.

Visit the Jossey-Bass Web site at **www.josseybass.com.**

Executive Summary

A critical synthesis of research literature on the process of organizational change at the institutional level is needed because higher education is being asked to be responsive to an ever-changing environment. This work focuses on providing the reader several key insights into the change process by (1) presenting a common language for organizational change; (2) describing the multidisciplinary research base on change; (3) highlighting the distinct characteristics of higher education institutions and how this might influence the change process; (4) reviewing models/concepts of organizational change derived within higher education, comparing and contrasting different approaches; and (5) providing principles for change based on a synthesis of the research within higher education.

Providing a Language for Understanding Organizational Change

Some generic definitions of organizational change have been offered by theorists. For example, Burnes noted that organizational change refers to understanding alterations within organizations at the broadest level among individuals, groups, and at the collective level across the entire organization (1996). Another definition is that change is the observation of difference over time in one or more dimensions of an entity (Van de Ven and Poole, 1995). But these definitions fail to capture the assumptions inherent in different models or theories of change. For example, cultural and social-cognition theories of change would replace the word *observation* with the word *perception* in the second definition above. Theorists exploring change through a cultural or social-cognition perspective would examine not dimensions (typically, organizational structural characteristics such as size), but values or organizational participants' mental maps. Because the language relating to change differs, a common language is difficult to find. However, certain concepts are common across various models, such as forces or sources of change and first-order or second-order change. These common concepts are noted within key sources of change literature such as Burnes, 1996; Goodman, 1982; Levy and Merry, 1986; and Rajagopalan and Spreitzer, 1996. As these scholars studied change, these concepts became critical points of concern in their analyses. Forces and sources examine the *why* of change. First and second/second order, scale, foci, timing, and degree all refer to the *what* of change. Adaptive/generative, proactive/reactive, active/static, and planned/unplanned refer to the *how* of change. Last, the target of change refers to the *outcomes*. As a campus begins to engage in a change process, members of the organization need to first examine why they are about to embark on the process, the degree of change needed, and what is the best approach to adopt.

Theories of Change

Six main categories of theories of change assist in understanding, describing, and developing insights about the change process: (1) evolutionary, (2) teleological, (3) life cycle, (4) dialectical, (5) social cognition, and (6) cultural. Each model has a distinct set of assumptions about why change occurs, how the process unfolds, when change occurs and how long it takes, and the outcomes of change. The main assumption underlying evolutionary theories is that change is a response to external circumstances, situational variables, and the environment faced by each organization (Morgan, 1986). Social systems as diversified, interdependent, complex systems evolve naturally over time because of external demands (Morgan, 1986). Teleological theories or planned change models assume that organizations are purposeful and adaptive. Change occurs because

Change occurs because leaders, change agents, and others see the necessity of change.

leaders, change agents, and others see the necessity of change. The process for change is rational and linear, as in evolutionary models, but individual managers are much more instrumental to the process (Carnall, 1995; Carr, Hard, and Trahant, 1996). Life-cycle models evolved from studies of child development and focus on stages of growth, organizational maturity, and organizational decline (Levy and Merry, 1986). Change is conceptualized as a natural part of human or organizational development. Dialectical models, also referred to as political models, characterize change as the result of clashing ideology or belief systems (Morgan, 1986). Conflict is seen as an inherent attribute of human interaction. Change processes are considered to be predominantly bargaining, consciousness-raising, persuasion, influence and power, and social movements (Bolman and Deal, 1991). Social-cognition models describe change as being tied to learning and mental processes such as sensemaking and mental models. Change occurs because individuals see a need to grow, learn, and change their behavior. In cultural models, change occurs naturally as a response to alterations in the human environment; cultures are always changing (Morgan, 1986). The change process tends to be long-term and slow. Change within an organization entails alteration of values, beliefs, myths, and rituals (Schein, 1985). Some researchers suggest using several models or categories, as each sheds light on different aspects of organizational life (Van de Ven and Poole, 1995). The advantage to multiple models is that they combine the insights of various change theories. Bolman's and Deal's (1991) reframing of organizations and Morgan's (1986) organizational metaphors illustrate how assumptions from teleological, evolutionary, political/cultural, social-cognition, and lifecycle models can be combined to understand change.

Understanding the Nature of Higher Education Organizations: Key to Successful Organizational Change

There are two main reasons it is necessary to develop a distinctive approach to change within higher education: overlooking these factors may result in mistakes in analysis and strategy, and using concepts foreign to the values of the academy will most likely fail to engage the very people who must bring about the change. In order to develop a distinctive model, the following unique features of higher education institutions need to be taken into account:

- Interdependent organization
- Relatively independent of environment
- Unique culture of the academy
- Institutional status
- Values-driven
- Multiple power and authority structures
- Loosely coupled system
- Organized anarchical decision-making
- Professional and administrative values
- Shared governance
- Employee commitment and tenure
- Goal ambiguity
- Image and success

Although not an exhaustive list, this represents some of the key features of higher education institutions that affect organizational change. (For a more detailed description of these characteristics, see Birnbaum, 1991.)

In light of these distinctive organizational features, higher education institutions would seem to be best interpreted through cultural, social-cognition, and political models. The need for cultural models seems clear from the embeddedness of members who create and reproduce the history and values, the stable nature of employment, the strong organizational identification of members, the emphasis on values, and the multiple organizational cultures. Because there are no bottom-line measures for examining performance in higher education, image and identification are extremely important in understanding if change is occurring and how it occurs. The relationships of image and identification to change seem to indicate that social cognition is important to understand. Furthermore, the loosely coupled structure, anarchical decision-making, and ambiguous goals make meaning unclear, and social-cognition models' emphasis on multiple interpretations may be important to consider when examining and facilitating change. The shared governance system, organized anarchy, conflicting administrative and professional values, and ambiguous, competing goals also point to a need for the interpretive power of political models. Evolutionary models are important for understanding the impact of environmental factors on change, such as accreditation, foundations, and legislatures in an interdependent system, especially since these factors are growing in magnitude and influence. However, even though a higher education institution is an open system, it may have internal consistency and logic that can be damaged by the intrusion of external environmental forces.

Higher Education Models of Change: Examination Through the Typology of Six Models

An extensive review of all the research on change conducted specifically within higher education, and within the framework of the six theories outlined above, provides a set of insights about the change process in this context. The cumulative evidence, so far, suggests that organizational change can best be explained through political, social-cognition, and cultural models. Political processes such as persuasion, informal negotiation, mediation, and coalition-building appear to be very powerful strategies for creating change (Conrad, 1978; Hearn, 1996). Social-cognition models illustrate the importance of altering mental models, learning, constructed interaction, and other processes for creating change (Eckel and Kezar, forthcoming; Weick, 1995). Cultural models demonstrate the importance of symbolism, history and traditions, and institutional culture for facilitating change on campus (Cohen and March, 1974; Kezar and Eckel, forthcoming). Evolutionary models highlight some key characteristics of change, such as homeostasis, interactivity of strategies, or accretion, that appear important to understanding change. Life-cycle models have not, for the most part, been applied to higher education institutions, but show promise for helping to develop explanations of how organizational change occurs. There is mixed evidence about the explanatory power of teleological models, but to date they appear to have limited support from the research in terms of how change actually occurs in higher education and of efficacy for facilitating change. Some strategies, such as incentives or vision, have proven successful for creating change.

Research-Based Principles of Change

A complex set of research-based principles emerges from this extensive review of the research. These principles include:

- Promote organizational self-discovery
- Be aware of how institutional culture affects change
- Realize that change in higher education is often political
- Lay groundwork for change
- Focus on adaptability
- Construct opportunities for interaction to develop new mental models
- Strive to create homeostasis and balance external forces with internal environment
- Combine traditional teleological tools such as establishing vision, planning, or strategy with social-cognition, cultural, and political strategies
- Be open to a disorderly process
- Facilitate shared governance and collective decision-making
- Articulate core characteristics
- Focus on image
- Connect the change process to individual and institutional identity
- Create a culture of risk and help people in changing belief systems
- Be aware that various levels or aspects of the organization will need different change models
- Realize that strategies for change vary by change initiative
- Consider combining models or approaches, as is demonstrated within the multiple models

These will help you to develop a systematic and systemic process of change that works with individuals, acknowledges change as a human process, is sensitive to the distinctive characteristics of higher education, is context-based, achieves balance of internal and external forces, and is open to creativity and leveraging change through chance occurrences.

Contents

Foreword

Understanding and effectively leading institutional change are central concerns for most of today's academic leaders, be they presidents, provosts, deans, student affairs professionals, or faculty. Institutional change has become an expected session at national association meetings and a familiar topic within the corridors of most, if not all, campus buildings. A number of well-articulated pressures are pushing institutional leaders to think more intentionally about making changes to better respond to a changing environment and to improve the quality of their institutions. Conventional wisdom about leading change abounds, such as the need for widespread involvement, thorough communication, and leadership. However, the new popularity of change as a topic has not rendered institutional change more deeply understood or more easily implemented.

Adrianna Kezar, a higher education faculty member at the University of Maryland, College Park, tackles the complex topic of institutional change in this monograph, *Understanding and Facilitating Organizational Change in the 21st Century: Recent Research and Conceptualizations.* She synthesizes a wide range of scholarly research on organizational behavior and change from inside and outside higher education, with the intent of identifying a set of principles that can deepen our understanding of the change process in higher education. This monograph is grounded in the assumption that institutional change is facilitated by better understanding the process of change from multiple perspectives. A comprehensive and nuanced understanding needs to draw upon a diverse literature, with its varying sets of assumptions, and requires a familiarity with the unique organizational characteristics of academic institutions.

A single approach to change may overlook essential elements and contain unarticulated assumptions. The complex ideas in this monograph, presented in a clearly organized framework, will help leaders make wise choices and develop strategies and approaches to effect desired change.

The volume is organized into five sections. First, Kezar presents a common language for organizational change. A clear comprehension of ideas and of how the various theorists' language of change converges and diverges is essential to a solid understanding of the complexity of change. Second, the author describes the wide-ranging and multidisciplinary change literature, drawing out assumptions and highlighting commonalities. Third, she reviews the distinctive characteristics of colleges and universities, and explores how these elements inform the change process. Without a solid grasp of organizational context, campus leaders may attempt to implement change processes inconsistent with the nature of their institutions. Fourth, she compares and contrasts important models of change presented in the higher education literature. Kezar concludes by offering a set of research-based principles for change.

The need to understand and facilitate institutional change is growing not only in the United States, but also abroad, making this work timely. Higher education in Europe and Canada is undergoing tremendous change. At a recent transatlantic meeting in Canada, sponsored by the American Council on Education and the European Universities Association, institutional leaders from Europe and North America agreed that one of their most important shared challenges was the need to bring about major institutional change. Institutional change is increasingly occupying the time and attention of academic leaders worldwide.

Peter D. Eckel
Associate Director for Institutional Initiatives
American Council on Education

Acknowledgments

This monograph is dedicated the many important people who help to create change in my own life because of their energy, spirit, and integrity: Tom Kezar, Monica Kezar, Dan Kezar, Tara Kezar +3, and Carol Kezar; and my dear, close friends Beth Minehart, Rachel Flanagan, Elizabeth Leinbach, Ginger Donnell, Maureen Vasquez, Stephanie Perkal, Michelle Gilliard, Jaci King, Kristen Winklerath, and Tami Goodstein. I also want to thank the staff at ERIC— Pat Wood, Lori Cavell, Tracy Boswell, Shannon Loane, Eugene Yuk, and Liz Miles—for being so wonderful to work with. I hope that these lessons have been implemented in our own workplace. Lastly, I want to thank the reviewers who provided valuable feedback and Peter Eckel for his support over the years as we have wrestled to understand the nature of change in higher education.

Understanding and Facilitating Organizational Change in the 21st Century: Recent Research and Conceptualizations

SEVERAL CONDITIONS have coalesced in recent years that necessitate a synthesis of the organizational change literature. There are more pronouncements of crisis in higher education today than ever before, coming from both within and outside of the academy (Birnbaum, 2000). Whether this is actually a time of crisis is debatable, yet it is clear that higher education faces a host of changes that can no longer be ignored. The list of transforming forces has become so common that it is almost unnecessary to name them—technology, new teaching and learning approaches such as community-service learning or collaborative learning, cost constraints, changing demographics, international competition, assessment, accountability, diversity/multiculturalism, and other challenges create a complex climate. (For a detailed look at each of these forces, see Green and Hayward, 1997.) These challenges have, in some cases, created stress in institutions (Green and Hayward, 1997; Leslie and Fretwell, 1996). Not only is change described as necessary based on external pressures, but also the sheer number of major changes keeps increasing (Green and Hayward, 1997; Leslie and Fretwell, 1996).

Some scholars describe the changing context as a reason to reexamine organizational structures and culture, necessitating internal change. Bergquist, for example, describes the postmodern era as posing new challenges for organizations, particularly around the issue of change (1998). Postmodernism requires organizations to change their size and shape to respond to a more fragmented and complex environment. Reexamining the institutional mission is a major priority (Bergquist, 1998; Cameron and Tschichart, 1992). As institutions rethink their reasons for being, the institutions themselves change their identities; Bergquist lists several institutional responses. First, the postmodern environment means that organizations move from more singular models of operation (as bureaucratic or as a research university) to examining multiple ways to be successful. Second, organizations might actively engage the various subcultures within higher education institutions, including the political, bureaucratic, symbolic, and human resource cultures. Third, other organizations might develop entrepreneurial cultures and structures in which they are able to adapt to changes. Last, they might find their distinctive niches, focusing on specialized aspects rather than a more comprehensive mission as higher education institutions have done in the past. Organizational change is conceptualized as an effort at becoming less homogenous and responsive to the multiplicity of various constituents (for example, women and people of color), customers, or interest groups. According to Bergquist, the postmodern era is requiring organizations to change; there is no way to avoid this cycle.

Another factor requiring an update to our knowledge base on organizational change is the plethora of new models developed and research conducted in the last decade. The Kellogg Foundation has funded several major studies on change and transformation within higher education, resulting in the creation of several research teams around the country that have developed new conceptualizations and strategies for change. In addition, the Pew Charitable Trusts Leadership Award, initiated in 1996, attempts to document institutions that have responded to calls for change in higher education, providing models for other institutions. The purpose of this project is to highlight successful change efforts and help more institutions realize the necessity of change. Institutions involved in the Pew project are required to illustrate change in curriculum, faculty roles, and resource allocation. The sheer number of calls for change by policy-makers has spawned interest from organizational theorists in further exploring the structures and attitudes that influence the change process. Although many individual publications are being developed, without synthesis of these various ideas, there is no way for practitioners to compare the advantages or disadvantages of various models and conceptualizations.

Finally, higher education administration programs have developed new courses on change or leadership classes in which organizational change is a major component. The growing number of classes in this area also requires that the knowledge base be collected and organized in one publication. Even if there were not calls for change, it would be necessary to synthesize this literature for students, faculty, and scholars. Although episodes of extreme change tend to be cyclical, anyone who has spent any time in organizations knows that change is ongoing. This knowledge is always needed for leading and working within higher education institutions.

Probably the single most important reason for readers to carefully review the information from the collective research knowledge base is the findings of research studies about change: using change strategies accurately has been demonstrated to affect the success or failure of an effort (Collins, 1998). The research also illustrates the important principle that one size does not fit all when it comes to change approaches—a principle commonly misunderstood among education professionals (Birnbaum, 1991a; Bolman and Deal, 1991). Solutions such as total quality management, interpretive strategy, or becoming a learning organization do not work within all environments, among all types of changes, or within all institutional structures and cultures. Yet professionals tend to use whatever change theory or approach they are familiar with or that is popular at the time. With many prominent scholars and opinion leaders calling for a serious examination of institutional structure, mission, and culture, and a plethora of new research and ideas, a better understanding and synthesis of knowledge about change seems appropriate.

> . . . professionals tend to use whatever change theory or approach they are familiar with or that is popular at the time.

Distinctive Contribution

This monograph presents a critical synthesis of research literature on the organizational change process at the institutional level, providing guidance about the strengths and weaknesses of different approaches or models and offering research-based principles. This differs from other resources that focus on one approach, such as reengineering, or nonresearch based models. Much of the organizational change literature has been written from the perspective of a writer who believes in one approach to facilitate change. Such writers often become advocates of a model, rather than providing careful, cautionary tales to readers about use of the approach. Also, the vast majority of the literature focuses on planned change; in fact, the last major review of change literature in higher education, by Robert Nordvall (1982) focused only on planned change. Although planned change is important to understand, much of the change that occurs is unplanned or only partially planned. Another weakness in the change literature is that the vast majority of literature relies on anecdotal change stories or cases such as *Introducing Change from the Top in Universities and Colleges: 10 Personal Accounts* (Weil, 1994). These voices can provide some insight, but tend to be idiosyncratic stories that can be applied to other situations and campuses with limited success. This report is distinctive in its focus on research.

Moreover, it focuses on organizational change rather than change agents. Many recent books review change agents' roles, examining how department chairs, deans, faculty, student affairs officers, and presidents can help to initiate change (Wolverton and others, 1998). These books tend to focus on particulars of a functional area. For example, change agents in academic affairs administration are briefed on the importance to change of tenure review processes, evaluation, faculty development, or hiring (Lucas and Assoc., 2000). Such resources for change agents provide some helpful strategies, yet they lack the broad, conceptual knowledge necessary to create and sustain change. Furthermore, these resources are based on experiences and anecdotes rather than research, so there is no proof that they work. At this point, no broad synthesis of the conceptual, research-based literature on the change process has been developed. This monograph attempts to fill that gap in our knowledge.

Focus of the Monograph

It is assumed that higher education institutions do change, yet we need to better understand how, why, and under what circumstances this occurs. The focus is on synthesizing the literature on all change models across the multidisciplinary fields that have studied change, examining these models in relation to the unique higher education environment, and trying to determine the relative merit of various approaches to studying and understanding change in higher education. This monograph focuses on change at the institutional level and will address state- and national-level studies only occasionally. For sources on state change, see Altbach, Berdhal, and Gumport (1998); for national systems, see Clark (1983a) and Sporn (1999). This work will not argue for the need to change. For an overview of the need for change or the literature on various changes currently facing the academy, see Green and Hayward (1997); Leslie and Fretwell (1996).

This monograph is organized in the following manner. Article two focuses on reviewing major terms or concepts related to change, such as first-order and second-order change, scale of change, and proactive versus reactive change. These terms are important for understanding change theories and beginning to develop a common language for change. One of the major difficulties related to change is that people have unspoken assumptions about how they define and think about change. This article provides some common concepts so that campus leaders can frame discussions about change and identify hidden assumptions. It also attempts to define what change is and distinguish it from diffusion, innovation, institutionalization, and other similar phenomena. It is important to realize that there are many different definitions of change and that these definitions are directly tied to different theories about change. Thus, there is no single definition offered in article two; instead, definitions are offered in article three in conjunction with theories of change.

Article three reviews the research on organizational change, from several disciplines including political science, anthropology, biology, physics, psychology, business, and management. Because the literature is so extensive, it is organized into major change theories according to a typology of six categories: evolutionary, lifecycle, teleological, political, social-cognition, and cultural models. This typology is an original contribution, but builds on the work of Van de Ven and Poole (1995). These categories of models/theories are described in terms of their definitions of change, major assumptions, examples of specific models, key players and activities, and benefits and criticisms. By understanding all major theories about change, leaders will be better equipped for facilitating the process.

Article four focuses on defining the unique characteristics of higher education institutions, relying heavily on the work of Robert Berdhal (1991), William Bergquist (1992), Robert Birnbaum (1991a), Burton Clark (1983a), and Karl Weick (1991). The change literature is analyzed in relation to characteristics that define higher education organizations as unique. Few scholars have examined change on college campuses as distinct from that in other organizations. Instead, models of change from other disciplines or used within other organizational types have been applied to higher education, without consideration of whether this transference is appropriate. The examination of the unique features of higher education in relation to change and observations made from this meta-analysis has the potential to develop approaches to change that are more successful.

In article five, the literature on change from the field of higher education is presented. The typology of change theories is used to organize this literature, allowing the reader to reflect on the key assumptions, benefits, and criticisms already presented. The results of studies directly applied within the higher education setting assist in understanding the efficacy of these models/theories, sometimes derived from outside the realm of higher education, for understanding organizational change. This article does more than synthesize the literature—it begins to create a vision for how change occurs in higher education.

In article six, the earlier articles are consolidated into a set of research-based principles for understanding and facilitating change in higher education. Rather than provide solutions or recommend a model for change, this monograph provides a set of principles that can be used to guide the change process. These principles are derived from the collective wisdom of hundreds of research studies. No recipe is offered; understanding change requires the development of a common language and conceptualization of change that is context based.

The monograph ends with suggestions for future research, article seven. We know less than we should about how change occurs in higher education. There have been few long-term or sustained research agendas by researchers or research projects. Instead, a researcher will conduct a study or two on change, then move on to another topic. Given the lack of consistent attention to this topic in higher education, there are many gaps in our knowledge that need exploration. Future areas for research are detailed, again organized by the typology of six models.

In summary, this work focuses on providing the reader key insights into the change process: (1) it provides a common language for organizational change by reviewing terminology; (2) it brings together the multidisciplinary research base on change; (3) it outlines the ways in which higher education is a distinct institutional type and how this might influence the change process; (4) it reviews models and concepts of organizational change derived from within higher education, comparing and contrasting different approaches; (5) it offers research-based principles for change; and (6) it presents areas in need of future research.

Audience

It is assumed that any member of the institution can be a change agent and can successfully use the principles listed in article six. In fact, acknowledging that any institutional member can be a change agent facilitates the change process. One of the core assumptions among many change models or conceptualizations is the importance of collective leadership. Therefore, it is hoped that all readers feel empowered to use the lessons in this monograph.

The audience for this work is quite broad. Academic leaders, such as deans and department chairs, should find this a helpful resource to complement books on institutionalizing post-tenure review or assessment, for example. This will help them to overcome barriers that these books are not likely to describe or aspects of the process that are not articulated. Staff members, often not familiar with academic traditions, will find this book insightful as to any distinctive characteristics of the higher education enterprise that may have eluded them. Many staff members come to higher education from the government or private industry and have difficulty understanding shared governance and faculty autonomy, for example. When staff members try to create changes related to the admissions process, faculty behavior might be difficult to understand. For upper-level administrators, presidents, trustees, and even policy-makers, this monograph offers insight into the way change occurs in higher education, which will challenge some of the current approaches to change, such as performance funding. Yet it reinforces other traditions such as accreditation or fostering local change, and it creates opportunities for suggesting new policy directions such as ways to develop environments for adaptability.

The main audience is members of college and university communities. Each individual can enhance their knowledge about change and learn a language that will help them to facilitate the process on campus. There are better sources for informing policy-makers and trustees, yet they can also benefit from the information synthesized and analyzed in this monograph. Higher education graduate students, faculty, and researchers are also a main audience for the monograph, as the mission of this series is to bring together our collective research knowledge on a topic. This monograph can serve as a text for courses on change and innovation in higher education.

To Change or Not to Change?

Although this volume brings together the collective knowledge base on change, the author acknowledges that higher education institutions are important social institutions that maintain timeless values and should be resistant to change that would endanger many of these important values. As a historian of higher education, I realize how vastly institutions have changed over the years—by admitting new populations, changing the nature of the curriculum, reorienting employee roles, or developing new administrative structures—but each of these changes occurred in distinctive ways, some planned and others evolved. This monograph is different from most of the literature on change; it advocates resistance to change as a healthy response. Readers should be clear on the fact that understanding the change process can be used to resist change as well as to encourage it.

Change is not always good, and it is certainly not a panacea for all the issues facing higher education. More leaders may need to prioritize various change proposals and defuse poor ideas, rather than always responding to changes from the internal and external environment. Therefore, failure to change can be a positive response. I am highly suspicious of the recent trends in business to reconfigure organizations every five years and of the idealization and symbolic value of change as a trophy of managerial success (Czarniawska and Sevon, 1996). Higher education institutions are tradition-bound, and continuity is an important feature. One of the reasons for higher education's success as an institution has been its ability to stay focused on its mission. Thus, this monograph is in no way intended to advocate change for change's sake. Change should be engaged in only if the environment legitimately challenges the organization's key mission or expertise. Furthermore, proactive change, rather than change led by the environment (as is the case in the health care industry), is usually in the best interest of higher education.

Zelda Gamson recently questioned the calls for change in higher education, asking which important aspects of higher education we should not change. She noted autonomy and community as important principles to be maintained (Gamson, 1999). What needs to be preserved may be just as important to understand as what needs to be changed. Another important plea is made by John Macdonald in his book, *Calling a Halt to Mindless Change*, written in response to the past two decades' literature on organizational change. This book notes that "executives should listen to the siren song of change with a healthy dose of skepticism" (MacDonald, 1997, p. viii). A main concept of MacDonald's book is a return to viewing change as evolutionary rather than declaring that every institution needs revolutionary change, the latter being a popular view in the management literature. The author suggests that the real pace of change is well within normal decision-making cycles. Calls for urgent revolutionary change are seen, for the most part, as scams created by management consultants to create a market for their knowledge. Although MacDonald may hold an extreme view, I think it is important for campuses to engage in a discussion about the need for and circumstances of change to ensure that the institution does not abandon important traditions that support excellence and performance. Balance between calls for change and tradition may be desirable.

Providing a Common
Language for Understanding
Organizational Change

EVERY FACULTY MEMBER in the school of business is being asked to use new technology in the classroom within the next three years, mirroring a trend for MBA programs across the country. (Example A)

An institution reduces costs suddenly by 20 percent redefines its mission, and serves a different student population. (Example B)

A department will begin faculty post-tenure review, reflecting the department's values change toward embracing assessment. (Example C)

Student affairs staff will redefine multiculturalism. (Example D)

Each of these statements describes a different type of organizational change and requires some examination and analysis before understanding which change model might work best. The purpose of this article is to briefly describe some of the common concepts related to organizational change, using the four examples listed above, that will make it easier to understand the conceptual literature described in articles three and five. The concepts will also help readers better categorize and understand changes on their campuses. The common language developed by reviewing these examples within this article refers to the why, what, and how of change, which comprise many essential elements of the models reviewed in the next article. Certainly, more detailed examples could be described that present institutional type and other contextual issues, but the purpose of the examples is limited to understanding the type of change.

Some readers might be thinking, why not directly obtain the literature on, for example, how student affairs divisions are handling multiculturalism? Such resources can indeed be useful. Members of an organization often feel they are equipped to move forward with change once they have examined the literature on the content or type of change, such as technology change. They may learn that distributed computing and increased specialization are key elements and that Internet connectivity is the most successful approach, but they will find little guidance on the process of change. Some content literature discusses process, but almost always in an atheoretical way or through only one model of change. Understanding the process of change is critical to successful implementation. Before examining the differences among the four change initiatives listed above, it is important to attempt to define change and to differentiate change from other similar phenomena.

What Is Organizational Change?

At this juncture in the monograph, this is a hard question to answer because the definition of organizational change varies by what model the reader uses to examine it. Some generic definitions have been offered in the research literature. For example, Burnes noted that organizational change refers to understanding alterations within organizations at the broadest level among individuals, groups, and at the collective level across the entire organization (1996). Another definition is that change is the observation of difference over time in one or more dimensions of an entity (Van de Ven and Poole, 1995). However, these definitions fail to capture the assumptions inherent in different models or theories of change. For example, cultural and social-cognition theories of change would replace the word *observation* with the word *perception* in the second definition above. Theorists exploring change through a cultural or social-cognition perspective would examine not dimensions (typically, organizational structural characteristics such as size), but values or organizational participants' mental maps. Specific definitions of organizational change will be addressed throughout article three. But before defining change, it is important to distinguish it from other similar phenomena. Thus, I will next describe innovation, diffusion, institutionalization, reform, and adaptation, and will illustrate how change is broader than these concepts.

Diffusion, Institutionalization, Adaptation, Innovation, and Reform

Most higher education administrators think in terms of institutionalization or diffusion rather than true change. Change may be foreign to many readers, even though they think they have been working on organizational change for years. Many professionals find themselves trying to capitalize on good ideas or noting trends in the environment that may affect their institution. They wonder, how can they make others adopt this idea? When thinking along these lines, they are typically thinking about diffusion. Diffusion is an important change strategy, but it is not a change model or an overall approach to change. The phases in most diffusion models include awareness (an individual is exposed to an innovation but lacks complete information about it), interest (the person seeks information about the innovation), evaluation (the individual applies the innovation to his or her present and anticipated future situation and decides whether to try it), trial (the individual uses it on a small scale), and adoption (the person decides whether to use the innovation on a large scale) (Rogers, 1995). Diffusion models tend to focus on individuals rather than whole organizations. They do not seek to change people or structures within an organization. Also, these models tend to rely on innovations. Change does not always entail trying something new; it may entail returning to traditional values or past practices. Most diffusion models are described in linear phases, but recent models critique these initial approaches and suggest that diffusion is a more complex process with stops and starts (Rogers, 1995). Diffusion models have received a great deal of attention in the area of technology, where innovations tend to occur at a rapid pace and adoption often happens at an individual level.

Institutionalization is distinct from change models as well. It examines only a part of the process; whether a change process or innovation alters the work of organizational participants over time (Curry, 1992). Institutionalization is often discussed as a change outcome, but it is also discussed as a process including three phases: (1) mobilization, whereby the system is prepared for change; (2) implementation, whereby the change is introduced into the system; and, (3) institutionalization, whereby the system becomes stable in its changed state. The interest in institutionalization stems from the many changes that have occurred but not been sustained in higher education, such as cluster colleges, portfolios, nonletter grades, experiential learning, self-paced learning, total quality management, and other innovations that have come and gone (Levine, 1980). Both diffusion and institutionalization are parts of particular change models; they do not represent distinctive change models in themselves. These two phenomena are important aspects of change models. They have become extremely popular in the literature because they respond to different challenges in the change process.

Adaptation is a narrow term that refers to change specifically within evolutionary change models, which will be discussed in article three. It refers to "modifications and alterations in organization or its components in order to adjust to changes in the external environment" (Cameron, 1991, p. 284). *Innovation* is also a narrow term, referring to a tangible product process or procedure within an organization that is new to a social setting, intentional in nature rather than accidental, not routine (for example, appointment of a new staff member must entail the creation of a new position), aimed at producing benefits (intentional destruction would not be innovation), and public in its effects (if an innovation has no discernible impacts on others in an organization, it would not be considered an innovation) (King and Anderson, 1995). There are several important resources on innovation within the higher education literature, including Levine, 1980; Lindquist, 1978. Much of the innovation literature was produced in the 1970s as a result of the experimentation that was occurring in institutional structures, such as curriculum reform and experimental colleges. *Reform* refers to an innovation that is typically exerted from the top of a system or organization, or from outside the organization. There is less literature on reform in higher education due to its decentralized, autonomous structure.

Although is difficult to clearly define what change is and to distinguish it from other similar phenomena, certain concepts—such as forces or sources of change and first-order or second-order change—are common across various models. These common concepts are noted within key sources of change literature, including Burnes, 1996; Goodman, 1982; Levy and Merry, 1986; Rajagopalan and Spreitzer, 1996. As these scholars studied change, such concepts became critical points of concern in their analysis and were used to frame the analysis of change. Forces and sources examine the *why* of change. First and second/second order, scale, foci, timing, and degree all refer to the *what* of change. Adaptive/generative, proactive/reactive, active/static, and planned/unplanned refer to the *how* of change. Last, the *target* of change refers to the outcomes. These concepts, which provide a common language and undergird the study of change, will be described next.

Forces and Sources

The sources or forces affecting a change process are important to understand, especially when trying to ascertain whether a change initiative is valid or efficacious (Rajagopalan and Spreitzer, 1996). Often, organizations become focused on the what or the how of change and forget to consider the why. Understanding why a change is taking place is an important beginning part of the change analysis and conversation. The two different forces or sources of change typically noted are (1) external environment and (2) internal environment (Burnes, 1996; Rajagopalan and Spreitzer, 1996). The external environment can play a large role in organizational change. The evolutionary model of change, described in the next article, focuses on the interaction between the external environment and an organization. This interaction is seen as the major impetus for change. Internal sources that are noted for initiating change include gathering of surplus resources, readiness and willingness of at least a dominant coalition to endure change, and transformational leadership. The planned-change literature tends to focus more on the internal environment and the need to change as a result of a new leader's vision, change agents, and the like (Carnall, 1995). Although planned change is often a response to external factors, the impetus for the change is usually internal.

Although planned change is often a response to external factors, the impetus for the change is usually internal.

In the case of example A above, we know that the source of change in technology is competition from other MBA programs across the country, an external force. Post-tenure review is being instituted in example C because of department values, an internal source. In example D, the force behind the movement in student affairs to redefine multiculturalism is unclear. In analyzing that situation we might ask what is the source of this change initiative and is it valid?

Degree of Change

One of the primary distinctions in the literature is between first- and second-order change (Goodman, 1982; Levy and Merry, 1986). First-order change involves minor adjustments and improvements in one or a few dimensions of the organization; it does not change the organization's core. Change occurs among individual or group levels. It is characterized by evolutionary change, a linear process, developmental or ongoing efforts, single-loop learning (allowing the organization to carry on its present policies or achieve its present objectives), and incremental approaches (Levy and Merry, 1986). For example, a first-order change might be changing a class in a department or creating a subunit within a university to carry out a responsibility such as service learning. Using the examples presented at the beginning of the article, post-tenure review is a first-order change because it fits into the program's existing values and structure. Much of the change described in the higher education literature is first-order change. First-order change is often associated with the theoretical perspective called *organizational development* (described in detail in article three).

Second-order change is transformational change; the underlying values or mission, culture, functioning processes, and structure of the organization change (Levy and Merry, 1986). The organization changes at its core, and the change is irreversible. Second-order change is often associated with a crisis that precipitates the change. Characteristics associated with second-order change are that it tends to be multidimensional (many aspects of the organization change); to be multilevel (individuals, groups, and the overall organization change); to be discontinuous; to seem irrational because the change is based on an unfamiliar logic or worldview; to involve double-loop learning (examining and altering mismatches in governing variables, which are preferred states that individuals strive to satisfy); and to result in a paradigmatic shift (Argyis, 1982; Levy and Merry, 1986). An example of second-order change would be to alter the reward structure for faculty to focus more on teaching rather than on research in research I universities. Second-order change can have two forms of resistance, from both within the organization and outside it. When change is too radical and the system is vastly different from its domain, the change threatens its environment and can generate strong resistance. Second-order change tends to be associated with a group of researchers working within the theoretical tradition called *organizational transformation* rather than with organizational development.

In the 1980s the notion of paradigmatic shift was extremely popular in organizational theory; this is an example of second-order change. A paradigm comprises the philosophy, beliefs, values, structures, policies, and operations that characterize an organization. Research on this subject evolved from Kuhn's theory of scientific revolution (Van de Ven and Poole, 1995). In more recent years, the applicability of paradigmatic shift has been questioned based on estimates that 90 to 95 percent of changes undertaken by organizations are not major changes in worldview (Burnes, 1996). Although some changes may be second order, multidimensional, and radical, few really involve a change in worldview. The focus on paradigmatic shift has lessened in the past decade.

More recent scholarship dissolves the dichotomy of first-order (incremental, fine-tuning, adjustments, development) and second-order (discontinuous or frame-breaking, transformation) change, examining a continuum or combination of change levels. Gersick (1991) describes the punctuated-equilibrium paradigm in which organizations are conceptualized as alternating between long periods of stable continuous change and adaptation and brief periods of revolutionary upheaval. He argues the prevalence of this approach across different theories and aspects of change: individual change (Levinson), organizations (Tushman, Newman, and Romanelli, 1986), scientific fields (Kuhn), biological species (Gould), and grand theory (Prigogine and Stengers).

Timing of Change

Scholars have also classified change as revolutionary or evolutionary in their attempts to classify differences in timing (Gersick, 1991; Levy and Merry, 1986). Revolutionary change departs significantly from the existing organization and usually occurs suddenly, with drastic changes within the mission, culture, and structure. Revolutionary change tends be associated with second-order change, but it occurs rapidly. In contrast, evolutionary changes are seen as natural—alteration of the mission happens over time. Culture changes as new people come into the organization, and structures change with the retention of new people adapting to the evolving mission. Evolutionary change is less likely to be adopted by leaders and change agents because it is seen as very long-term, sometimes jeopardizing an organization's ability to be responsive to its external environment. However, some researchers argue that revolutionary change can tragically damage the organization. As a result, researchers are also arguing for a continuum of timing, suggesting that much planned change is neither revolutionary nor evolutionary (Levy and Merry, 1986). Being cognizant of the dangers of different timing in change processes is important. For example, the post-tenure review process that is gradually building on another initiative (example C) is an evolutionary change, whereas the college that suddenly cuts costs and alters its mission and enrollments (example B) experiences revolutionary change.

Scale of Change

The scale of change has been examined through frameworks that divide the organization into understandable parts for investigation, such as individual, interpersonal, and organizational levels (Goodman, 1982). Some models examine or focus on only one of these levels, but most touch on all three. It is considered more theoretically sound if the researcher examines organizational change through all three levels (Bergquist, 1992). Another level that has begun to be examined is the scale of change at the industry or enterprise level, not just the organizational level. The following scheme has been developed: (1) adaptation (firm-level, first-order change); (2) metamorphosis (firm-level, second-order change); (3) evolution (industry-level, first-order change); and (4) revolution (industry-level, second-order change) (Meyer, Brooks, and Goes, 1990).

Adopting technology into classrooms to compete with other MBA programs is an evolutionary, industry-level, first-order change. The technology integration would be mostly an individual-level change. At this point, about 130 schools have adopted post-tenure review, so this represents an adaptation for schools. Post-tenure review affects all three levels, as institutional policies are changed to encompass a new process. Interpersonal dynamics are affected because colleagues, in addition to the department chair and individual faculty member, often partake in the process. However, the institution that reduced costs and changed its mission (example B) went through a metamorphosis. This metamorphosis also affected all three levels: individual, interpersonal, and organizational scale.

Focus of Change

Focus of change refers to the issue of which aspects of the organization are affected by the change. Scale examined levels within and beyond the organization, whereas focus identifies the phenomena affected. A framework conceived by Watson describes three main foci: structure, process, and attitude (Bergquist, 1992). *Structure* refers to the organizational chart, the reward system, or institutional policies and procedures. In contrast, *process* relates to the way people interact within existing structures. *Attitude* focuses on how people feel about working within the existing structures and processes of the organization. Change in attitude is also tied to change in culture. Thus change can be a reflection of one, two, or all of these different aspects. Some models of change focus on one aspect more than another. For example, many scientific management models focus on a change in processes, whereas evolutionary models focus on structure and cultural or social-cognition models concentrate on attitude. It is important to consider these different foci of change as the theories are reviewed. Some argue that a change in structure without a change in attitude does not "really" reflect change (Senge, 1990). Changes can also be classified along these lines in terms of the content of change: faculty contracts or merit pay, for example, relate to structural changes; collaborative management represents a new process; and becoming more student-centered or having a more intellectual environment might be an attitude change with no structural or process changes. Structural changes are often characterized as being easier and less controversial than process or attitude changes.

Integrating technology into the classroom is a structural, process, and attitude issue, but mostly reflects a process change. Student affairs staff redefining multiculturalism is an attitude change, but it may also affect structures and processes over time. It is difficult to change any one of these foci without affecting the others, but the relative emphasis on each varies with the circumstances of change.

Adaptive/Generative

Change models have also been classified in terms of responsiveness. Adaptive change tends to be a one-time response to the external environment. Adaptive models also suggest that we cannot predict the future and must constantly reforecast. Changes are cyclical, responding to new forecasts. Senge argues that organizations in today's ever-changing environment must be generatively focused (1990). Generative change is ongoing and is reflected within the learning organization model. He suggests that generative change allows for second-order and revolutionary change to occur more easily (Senge, 1990). Post-tenure review, as in example C, is a generative change— it builds on existing change and is part of an ongoing process. In example B, the institution with a redefined mission made an adaptive change. Changes that result from continual learning may be more aligned with the institutional mission than adaptive changes that can alter institutional direction, creating long-term problems. What if the institution in example D redefines multiculturalism in student affairs as a response to a conference presentation, essentially making assumptions about the future but being unable to predict it? As a result of this adaptive change, the division could become out of sync with the larger institution, creating tension.

Intentionality: Planned Versus Unplanned Change

Another major difference in change efforts hinges on planned versus unplanned change. *Planned* or *managed change* refers to modifications that are deliberately shaped by organization members. Change experts inside or outside the organization focus on helping individuals to cope with the difficulties and implement efforts. Most research in the area of business and management focuses on planned change, which is the conscious decision to change, marked by the following characteristics: intentionality and deliberateness of process, involvement of internal and external expertise, and strategy of collaboration (Carr, Hard, and Trahant, 1996). Evolutionary change and accidental change are not considered planned change. Some researchers also note that unplanned change can increase adaptability and should not necessarily be seen as separate from planned change (Weick, 1979).

Three out of the four changes noted at the beginning of this article appear to be planned changes. Example B—the reduction in expenses, redefinition of mission, and serving of a different student population—may have also been planned, but it may well have occurred with limited planning. Some of the other changes may not have been planned; for example, the technology usage in the classroom may have just happened ad hoc.

Response Time: Proactive and Reactive

Change has also been classified as proactive (happening before a crisis) or reactive (happening after a crisis). Example B is an illustration of an institution that was most likely reactive, responding to a crisis. Planned change can be both reactive and proactive. Much of the literature cites the benefit of proactive change, which can be facilitated by a generative environment with ongoing learning (Argyis, 1982; Senge, 1990; Steeples, 1990). Examples A and C reflect the proactive process of change. In 2001, integration of computer technology into the classroom is not ahead of the curve, yet the institution in example A is not waiting until it is negatively affected to market its program to students. The post-tenure review change in example C appears to be proactive, as few institutions have made this change. However, this organization may be located in a state that has mandated post-tenure review. In that situation, the participants are being reactive, perhaps having less time to develop a careful response.

Active and Static

Change can be active (requiring many of the organizational participants to be involved) or static (one or a few individuals can implement the change). Technology integration, for instance, might happen autonomously at the classroom level and not require all individual staff members and administrators to be involved. But in other cases, conversion to new technology may be an intensely active process. None of the scenarios outlined at the beginning of this article seem to reflect static change, examples of which might include changing a budget report's format or making an alteration in a class. The post-tenure review process could be a static change; the dean may have made the decision and had two or three department chairs implement the change.

Target of Change: Change Process and Outcomes

Change models all describe process and outcomes. *Process* refers to the way in which change happens. Adaptive, generative, proactive, reactive, planned, and unplanned are different characterizations of the process of change. Each model described in the next article refers to assumptions about the process of change. Many variations of the change process have been referred to already, but it is important to connect the process to the outcomes of change.

Change outcome is a hotly debated area, especially in regard to whether outcomes are measurable, whether they should be measured or assessed at all, and whether only intended outcomes should be examined (Burke, 1995; Dawson, 1994; Eckel, Hill, Green, and Mallon, 1999; Huber and Van de Ven, 1995). Some scholars examine outcomes as the targets of change, including new structures, processes, missions, rituals, and individual beliefs. Others note that the outcome is not a specific aspect of the organization and argue that the change outcome is the overall change in the culture, meaning that outcomes are difficult to measure (Neumann, 1993; Schein, 1985). Still others view outcomes more qualitatively, based on whether the change brought benefits to the organization and the magnitude of any benefits (Goodman, 1982). As noted earlier, institutionalization can be a change outcome.

In example A, the MBA program can survey faculty members to find out how many are using technology. But without a program evaluation, the benefits (outcome) will be unclear. In example B, the outcome of this institution's revolutionary metamorphosis is unclear, but an unintended outcome might be lowered morale. Redefining multiculturalism (example D) may result in a host of unintended outcomes. Change agents need to be aware of both intended and unintended outcomes as well as ways to identify the complex sets of outcomes that can result from the change process.

Summary

This article presented some of the key concepts and terms that will be found within all the theories of organizational change reviewed in the following articles. The concepts emerged to respond to different questions about change. Forces and sources examine the *why* of change. First and second/second order, scale, foci, timing, and degree all refer to the *what* of change. Adaptive/ generative, proactive/reactive, active/static, and planned/ unplanned refer to the *how* of change. Last, the *target* of change refers to the outcomes. Understanding which questions to ask in order to frame the analysis of change is the first step. Now the reader can begin to examine each change situation on their own campus in terms of why, what, how, and outcomes. Furthermore, this article provided the kind of language needed to meaningfully discuss change with colleagues and to interpret the ways in which other people describe change.

Change agents need to be aware of both intended and unintended outcomes as well as ways to identify the complex sets of outcomes that can result from the change process.

Theories and Models
of Organizational Change

WHY ARE MODELS of organizational change necessary or important to understand? They are helpful for assessing change at a macro level—the level at which many institutional leaders view (or should view) their organizations. Models can reveal why change occurs (the driving forces of change); how change will occur (the stages, scale, timing, and process characteristics); and what will occur (the content of change, outcomes, and ways to measure it). In addition, each model of change represents a different ideology with its own assumptions about the nature of human beings and social organizations. For example, can people change easily, or do they have fairly rigid identities? Most models address the question of determinism: Is change beyond the capacity of people to manage and shape? Choosing a model is not an arbitrary choice—it is an ideological one. The assumptions we make about change are also assumptions about the nature of reality and people. It is important to review the multidisciplinary research on change because some of the ideas have not been applied in higher education. Furthermore, each model helps us to understand different aspects of change. This article reviews the six main typologies of organizational change.

Typology of Organizational Change Models

Many different theories/models of organizational change exist throughout the multidisciplinary literature base.[1] The literature referred to in this section will be limited to organizational change models rather than human, biological, or grand change theories (Phillips and Duran, 1992; Salipante and Golden-Biddle, 1995). In this section, six categories of change models are discussed, with each category encompassing many different individual models. Since there is such a proliferation of individual models, these categories serve as an organizing device. This monograph uses some traditional typologies and proposes a few new categories based on the current literature (Dill and Helm, 1988; Van de Ven and Poole, 1995).

One of the most comprehensive typologies, offered by Van De Ven and Poole, employs the following categories: life cycle, evolutionary, dialectical, and teleological (1995). Two additional categories that have been suggested are social-cognition and cultural approaches to change. Some theorists argue that life-cycle models are a variation of evolutionary models, but there appears to be enough evidence to distinguish between them (Levy and Merry, 1986). For example, life-cycle models emerge from a different disciplinary base (psychology rather than biology), are less deterministic, and focus more on the human elements of change, among other distinctions. Nordvall's last synthesis (1982) described only eight models within three categories: (1) teleological models such as problem-solving, action research, and organizational development; (2) dialectical models such as political models and social interaction; and (3) evolutionary models such as systems theory and adaptive models. The individual models now number in the hundreds and are difficult to synthesize. Authors are developing change classification schemes within individual categories such as evolutionary or teleological models (Van de Ven and Poole, 1995). These two

---

[1] *Model* and *theory* are not necessarily interchangeable words, although many scholars use them as such. In fact, *theory* suggests abstract contemplation or insight, whereas *model* connotes a set of plans or procedures. Certain disciplines (such as business or psychology) tend to develop models, while other fields (such as the sciences) tend to discuss theories of change. I will use *model* as the general term within this monograph. Most scholars hold that no theory of change has yet been developed.

categories, in particular, have a proliferation of individual models, requiring more refined categorization (Phillips and Duran, 1992).

Most prevalent in the literature are the teleological (scientific management or planned change) and evolutionary (adaptive change) models. These two approaches have the longest histories and have been embraced by many practitioners and researchers as useful for understanding change. Most current critiques refer to the recurring debate between planned change and adaptive models, as they are commonly referred to in the literature. These models also have the most starkly contrasting assumptions, as will be described in more detail below. Briefly, they represent dichotomies such as materialist/idealist, social/technical, intentional/deterministic, and subjective/objective, with planned change reflecting the first set of characteristics in these dichotomies and adaptive change reflecting the second set. Two authors note that there is "a comfort in the fact that the two schools criticize each other leading to improvements and achieving a kind of balance" (Czarniawska and Sevon, 1996, p. 14). They further express the concern that the two theoretical perspectives appear to have reached a stalemate that needs to be broken. The "garbage can" model offered by Cohen and March is one theory that emerged as a result of an earlier stalemate between these two models, accepting both contingency and control as shaping the process of change (1991a, 1991b). Social-cognition, dialectical, and cultural models evolved out of efforts to reconcile some of the perceived problematic assumptions of planned change and adaptive change models.

> **Most prevalent . . . are the teleological (scientific management or planned change) and evolutionary (adaptive change) models.**

The literature will be discussed using the following framework within each category: (1) major assumptions of this category of models (why change occurs, the process, the outcomes, key metaphor); (2) some examples of each model; (3) key activities or individuals; and (4) benefits and criticisms of the model. The difficulty with any typology is that each of the particular models has unique characteristics that cannot all be reflected within this discussion. However, the similarities among models in different categories are perhaps more significant than the differences. Some teleological models, for instance, share assumptions with evolutionary models. Some scholars consider strategic choice to be teleological, while others view it as evolutionary; likewise, paradigm-reframing models often overlap with social-cognition models, but some theorists see both as cultural models (Burnes, 1996; Collins, 1998). In effect, paradigm-reframing models share assumptions of both social-cognition and cultural approaches. Examples of models that share the assumptions of more than one category include organization punctuated equilibrium, community ecology, partisan mutual adjustment, and the "garbage can." The six categories described below, however, have fairly independent assumptions and ideologies that provide insight into understanding organizational change. A summary of all six models is provided in Appendix 1. The end of this article reviews combined models—approaches that utilize assumptions from several different theories. Combined models are particularly helpful because they capture insights from multiple studies of change.

Evolutionary

There are two main types of evolutionary models: social evolutionary models and biological models.

There are two main types of evolutionary models: social evolutionary models and biological models. Many individual models have developed within this tradition: adaptation, resource dependence, self-organization, contingency and systems theory, strategic choice, punctuated equilibrium, and population ecology. I use the term *evolutionary* throughout this monograph for simplicity's sake, but many scholars use the term *environmental theories* to encompass this set of concerns.

Major assumptions: The earliest ideas, based on biological investigations of change, focused on change as a slow stream of mutations, gradually shaped by environmental influences (Morgan, 1986). These were expanded by social evolutionary theories reflected in disciplines such as political science and sociology. The main assumption underlying all these theories is that change is dependent on circumstances, situational variables, and the environment faced by each organization (Morgan, 1986). Social systems as diversified, interdependent, complex systems evolve over time naturally (Morgan, 1986). But evolution is basically deterministic, and people have only a minor impact on the nature and direction of the change process (Hrebiniak and Joyce, 1985). These models focus on the inability of organizations to plan for and respond to change, and their tendency to instead "manage" change as it occurs. The emphasis is on a slow process, rather than discrete events or activities (Kieser, 1989). Change happens because the environment demands change for survival. Some later models suggest that adaptation can be proactive and anticipatory (Cameron, 1991). The assumptions in these theories range from managers having no ability to influence adaptability to managers having significant ability to be proactive, anticipating changes in the environment (March, 1994a).

Key concepts include systems, interactivity between the organization and its environment, openness, homeostasis, and evolution (Morgan, 1986). Evolution has already been described herein; the other terms can be clarified as follows. The concept of *systems* reflects how organizations are perceived as having interdependent and interrelated structures. Changing one part of the structure has implications for other parts. *Interactivity* is similar to systems in terms of focusing on the connected nature of activities within organizations. Based on the notions of systems and interactivity, change is conceptualized as reaching throughout an organization rather than being isolated. *Openness* refers to the relationship between the environment and internal transformation, and tends to characterize change as highly dependent on the external environment. Open systems exhibit an interdependence between internal and external environments. The concept of *homeostasis* refers to self-regulation and the ability to maintain a steady state by constantly seeking equilibrium between the system and environment (Sporn, 1999). Based on the principle of homeostasis, first-order change has been shown to be more common; yet, as was mentioned in article two, gradual change can be associated with occasional second-order change (graduated punctuation models).

Self-producing and self-organizing organisms form a key metaphor for change. Morgan (1986) uses the metaphor of termites for the change process within evolutionary models. Termites constantly rebuild their nest. This model presents a systemic, rational approach of a stimuli-and-response cycle. The process is unplanned and reactive. Processes include developing sensors (structures to determine necessary change and ability to adapt to new realities); determining organizational fitness; self-organizing; and local adaptation (Morgan, 1986). There is a strong structural emphasis in these models; the outcome of change is usually new organizational structures or organizing principles. Environmental leaders scan the environment to discern new developments and construct new units. Yet processes are inherently less important within evolutionary models than in other models, and change is mostly unplanned—instead it is an adaptive or selection-based process. Over time, it has become commonplace to assume that the environment affects the structure and culture of an organization, but this was a contested issue up until twenty years ago, when these models were being developed.

An example of the contribution of these models might be helpful. Prigogine details how, as organizations become more coherent and their structures more set (mature), they become more unstable and likely to experience second-order change. Managers' natural reaction to the resulting systems fluctuation is to try to restore order or stasis. But Prigogine's research illustrates that fluctuations are important for reestablishing order and that managers should let the open system follow its natural course rather than intervene (Levy and Merry, 1986). Note that these models de-emphasize action and focus on awareness of environmental influences and impacts so that the system can survive and be maintained.

Examples: The earliest examples of evolutionary models are modified theories of natural selection applied to organizational change. Later, unique models developed, such as the resource-dependence model. Within resource-dependence models, leaders make choices to adapt to their environment. The organization and its environment have an interdependent relationship, and the analytical focus is on transactions that occur as part of this relationship. This model differs from natural selection in its focus on leaders as active agents able to respond to and change the environment (Goodman, 1982). Resource-dependence theory presupposes that organizations are not self-sustaining and do need to rely on external resources; organizations are dependent on other organizations, leading to an interorganizational and political view (Sporn, 1999). Mergers are an example of organizational response to outside forces. This approach generated great interest, as it stresses a more interactive evolutionary model under which human agency can affect the change process.

Some models of strategy are also reflected within the evolutionary tradition, focusing on the effect of the environment. For example, in the strategic choice approach, managers can choose which environments they operate within, scanning, predicting changes, and steering the course of the organization (Cameron, 1991). Population-ecology models are also reflected within this tradition, examining how decisions and actions made by groups of organizations affect their survival and success. This model focuses on environmental niches and the relative success of specialist organizations or generalist populations under change forces such as diminished resources or loss of support for certain organizational activities. One notion that has developed from this theory is diversification—that is, the idea that generalist organizations perform better under certain environmental conditions because they have "diverse" customers, products, and services, and thus are less likely to feel the impact of changes in one part of the market. This type of adaptation can only be seen when viewed at the population level; hence the term *population ecology.*

A recent revival of evolutionary models of change applies chaos theory to change, as popularized by Margaret Wheatley in her book *Leadership and the new science: Discovering order in a chaotic world* (1999). Change is seen as inherent to biological systems; all organizations are constantly changing. The emphasis, as in earlier open-systems models, is on being aware of solutions inherent in the system through feedback loops, resiliency, and self-organizing, allowing structures to emerge within the system. Chaos models suggest that planned change is mostly irrelevant and unhelpful, and that organizations should respond organically to environmental demands.

Key activities or individuals: As may already be apparent, the key activities within this model include observation of the external environment, analysis of the organizational system, and creation of structures and new organizing principles to respond to the environment. Individual human agency tends to be de-emphasized within chaos models.

Benefits and criticisms: The contribution of these theories should not be underestimated. Illustrating the impact of context and environment on change was a radical approach in the face of scientific management theory, which examined organizations as self-contained entities (Morgan, 1986). It was also novel to describe change as unplanned. Reconceptualizing organizations as systems also advanced our thinking about change, identifying new reasons for and approaches to change. Many empirical studies illustrate the strength of evolutionary models for certain types of changes (Burnes, 1996; March, 1994a; Phillips and Duran, 1992; Sporn, 1999). Another advantage is the strong empirical research tradition that is not characteristic of many of the other theories.

Several concerns have been raised about chaos models' ability to explain organizational change, in particular, because they originated in mathematical rather than human-based fields. A substantial criticism is that these theories do not recognize that organizations are social phenomena, and thus they fail to provide needed assumptions about human psychology, the organization of work, and the way organizations fit into society (Collins, 1998). These models reflect little human agency; strategic choices and creativity are mostly unimportant. The models' overly deterministic nature and overemphasis on the impact of the environment are seen as problematic. A second concern is that it is difficult to directly link environment variables and organizational change, controlling all other variables. Therefore, these theories ignore important indirect and informal variables, and disregard the complexity of organizational life by focusing on a few factors within the external and internal environment, such as resources and size of organization (Burnes, 1996). Environmental turbulence and constraints are overemphasized, and the fact that these forces can be manipulated rather than merely adapted to is rarely mentioned (Burnes, 1996). These are major shortcomings that limit the explanatory power of evolutionary models. Despite these limitations, they are the second most popular category of models within the literature.

This category has several different common names, including planned change, scientific management, and rational models.

Teleological

This category has several different common names, including planned change, scientific management, and rational models. Strategic planning, organizational development, and adaptive learning approaches come under the teleological umbrella. These theories emerged simultaneously with the evolutionary models.

Assumptions: It is assumed that organizations are purposeful and adaptive. Change occurs because leaders, change agents, and others see the necessity of change. The process for change is rational and linear, as in evolutionary models, but individual managers are much more instrumental to the process (Carnall, 1995; Carr, Hard, and Tranant, 1996). Internal organizational features or decisions, rather than the external environment, motivate change. As noted earlier, these models are subjective and reflect intentionality. Key aspects of the change process include planning, assessment, incentives and rewards, stakeholder analysis and engagement, leadership, scanning, strategy, restructuring, and reengineering (Brill and Worth, 1997; Carnall, 1995; Huber and Glick, 1993). At the center of the process is the leader, who aligns goals, sets expectations, models, communicates, engages, and rewards. Strategic choices and human creativity are highlighted (Brill and Worth, 1997). Goal formation, implementation, evaluation, and modification based on experience are an ongoing process. New additions to the repertoire of management tools include collaborative culture definition, large group engagement processes, and individual in-depth interventions (Brill and Worth, 1997). The outcome of the change process is similar to that in evolutionary models: new structures or organizing principles. The metaphor for this model would be the change-master, to use Rosabeth Kanter's image (1983). The leader is the focus; this is a human model with the change agent at the center, using rational scientific management tools. This is the area with by far the most research and models.

Examples: Perhaps the best-known strategy within the teleological tradition is organizational development (Golembiewski, 1989; Goodman, 1982). This extensive body of research and literature dating from the 1950s continues today. Organizational development tends to address first-order change and does not challenge current organizational paradigms. It starts by diagnosing the problems within the organization on an ongoing basis (so it is generative) and searching for solutions (change initiatives). Goals are set for addressing the change, yet there is a heavy cultural emphasis on values, attitudes, and organizational norms. Many group meetings are conducted to help the change initiative develop momentum and to overcome resistance (Carr, Hard, and Trahant, 1996). The individual factors that inhibit change are a major emphasis; an analysis of obstacles is typically conducted. Organizations proceed through distinct stages, and it is the leaders' role to effectively manage the transition from one stable state to another (Golembiewski, 1989). Transition is a homogenous, structured, step-by-step process.

Another very popular scientific management approach is continuous quality improvement, or total quality management (TQM), which emerged from studies of how to improve the manufacturing sectors of U.S. businesses struggling to compete with Japanese companies. These models assume that change is prevented because institutions are based on long-standing traditions, practices, and values. Authors within this tradition point out that most organizations pursue quality, but that they have not examined the obstacles that prevent the change necessary to create quality, such as embedded values and structural or cultural hindrances (Freed, Klugman, and Fife, 1997). In order to challenge these barriers to change, a set of principles has been developed for leaders who create a new quality culture. Principles include many typical teleological strategies, such as (1) develop and focus on the vision, mission, and outcomes of the institution; (2) creative and supportive leadership; (3) retrain individuals on an ongoing basis or implement systematic individual development; (4) make data-driven decisions based on facts; (5) ensure collaboration; (6) delegate decision-making; and (7) proactively plan change. Quality experts say that they use "scientific management measurements and techniques" to alter personal philosophies and create a new organizational culture (Freed, Klugman, and Fife, 1997, p. 44). There is an assumed plasticity among people. TQM does adopt assumptions from biological theories in taking a systems approach, but the overall principles reflect the teleological tradition.

Reengineering focuses on modifying aspects of the organizational structure as the key to creating change (Barrow, 1996; Guskin, 1996). The leader's role is to inventory and assess the organizational structures, and to think about ways to structure differently. Mapping processes is a key management technique for helping to reengineer, which entails cross-functional teams meeting for extended periods of time to describe and chart a process from beginning to end. All divisions involved hear the processes of other functional areas and identify ways that processes can be collectively altered. Technology advancements, new products, retrained employees, cost-cutting, and other changes are facilitated by leaders who create a technology office, provide a new human resources office, or reduce the number of offices in charge of a particular function.

Key activities or individuals: This model sees change agents and leaders as the focus of the change process. Individuals within the organization receive little attention and are mostly unimportant. More recent teleological models, such as TQM and reengineering, involve individuals throughout the organization in the process of change through the use of teams and an emphasis on collaboration. Even though teleological models are broadening their focus, evolutionary and teleological models place the least emphasis on individuals throughout the organization as active participants. The activities for creating change are organized by the leader who plans, analyzes, and assesses. Activities are extremely important in these models, given the major assumption that management techniques or tools are the critical aspect for ensuring change.

Benefits and criticisms: The benefits of these models are significant. First, strategies for analyzing and categorizing change processes (for example, adaptive or generative) have been developed through these approaches, as described in article two. Second, the key role of leadership and change agents in the change process was identified and made apparent. Third, the role of collaboration and staff development are key concepts that have transformed our understanding of each organizational member's contribution to the change process. The emphasis on the role of people and individual attitudes to the change process was brought to the forefront, especially in research on resistance to change. The ability to, at times, forecast or identify the need for change was an important contribution, helping organizations to survive and prosper in what otherwise would have been difficult times.

There is a great deal of literature critiquing teleological models, probably because they tend to be the dominant model within the literature. But they have been tested, and their relevance for certain types of change has been proven through several studies (Freed, Klugman, and Fife, 1997; Levy and Merry, 1986). The main criticisms relate to the overly rational and linear process of change described within many teleological models (Dufty, 1980). Researchers of second-order change demonstrate a chaotic process and find management models to be lacking needed information on the importance of culture and social cognition. Another major criticism is the overemphasis on human creativity, thoughts, and decisions. In contrast, evolutionary studies of change have found that humans can create problems rather than assist in change processes (Levy and Merry, 1986). Furthermore, research has illustrated that organizations are often irrational, events happen spontaneously, environments change without predictability, control is illusory, and leaders' ability to change is more attributed than real.

There is also an assumed plasticity among people. Managers can alter the environment, and people can and will respond. Many of our own personal experiences might suffice to challenge this assumption (Collins, 1998). Studies of change have also illustrated how it tends to be continuous and open-ended (Burnes, 1996). Teleological models assume that organizations exist in a somewhat stable point and that managers can lead it from one set state to another. Others note that planned change models seem unable to address radical or transformation change (Schein, 1985). Teleological theorists within the continuous-improvement and learning-organization traditions feel they have addressed the criticisms that have been raised over time about second-order and continuous change (Senge, 1990).

Another critique is methodological in nature. Very few teleological studies examine change contextually; they ignore the substance of change, the need for change, and the politics of change (Pettigrew, 1985). It is noted that advice offered from generic prescriptions is therefore applied inappropriately, often creating problems.

Life Cycle

These models share many assumptions with evolutionary models in terms of adaptation and a systems approach. They differ in being less objective, focusing on the importance of human beings in the change process, and viewing changes that occur within the life cycles of people as well as those of the organizations they create. Life-cycle or developmental models emphasize systematic individual change.

Life-cycle or developmental models emphasize systematic individual change.

Assumptions: Life-cycle models evolved from studies of child development and focus on stages of organizational growth, maturity, and decline (Levy and Merry, 1986). Some scholars view life-cycle and developmental models as a branch of evolutionary models that focus on human development theories rather than broad biological theories (Van de Ven and Poole, 1995). Within these models, change is typically seen as part of a stage and is progressive and rational (Miller and Friesen, 1980). Organizations are born, then they grow, mature, go through stages of revival, and eventually decline (Goodman, 1982). Change does not occur because people see the necessity of or even want change; it occurs because it is a natural progression that cannot be stopped or altered (Miller and Friesen, 1980; Morgan, 1986). Developmental models focus on stages that are less predetermined than those in life-cycle models.

Change occurs as individuals within the organization adapt to its life cycle. Management is much more central than in evolutionary models and assists members of the organization to grow through training and motivational techniques (Rajagopalan and Spreitzer, 1996). The environment is ambiguous and threatening within this model. To adjust to this environment, processes include training and development, communication, and other structures that allow growth (Bolman and Deal, 1991; Miller and Friesen, 1980). The outcome within this change process is a new organizational identity. Identity is strongly emphasized in these models as a reason that people resist change (Van de Ven and Poole, 1995). Identification with the organization and personalization of work is also referenced. The major metaphor is the teacher or guide. Change is the result of staff development and leaders who bring people along to organizational maturity.

Life-cycle models are related to, but different from, learning models— learning is more adaptive, habitual, and regulated by nature (Burnes, 1996). Theories that focus more on learning and unlearning habits would fit within the life-cycle category. Some recent models of emotional intelligence and adaptability to change also fall within the life-cycle model (Collins, 1998). For example, certain abilities make one more able to or open to change, such as sensitivity to the motivations and perspectives of others (often termed *emotional intelligence*).

Examples: Grener describes a model of organizational growth through creativity, direction, delegation, coordination, and collaboration. Organizations go through five stages: high growth, greatest efficiency, diseconomies of scale, crisis, and last, transformation or cessation of functioning (Levy and Merry, 1986). High growth is stage in which an organization is building and there is a great deal of learning and experimenting; it models the youth and adolescence of a human life. Greater efficiency is like early adulthood, when the company has energy, momentum, and employees with high levels of training; it operates with a high profitability margin. Diseconomy of scales happens as the organization grows larger, participants show less commitment, and people become embedded in traditions or history, creating an environment in which the organization's productivity is lowered. If this stage is sustained, the organization often moves into crisis, losing profitability and success. At this point, typically, transformation occurs or the organization eventually stops functioning. Each stage ends in a crisis, which propels the organization into the next stage. Change occurs both within the stage (first order) and at the crisis point (second order). Life-cycle models characterize certain types of changes as typical within particular parts of the life cycle. For example, change in process is typical in the maturation phase, while change in structure is common with the centralization process. These patterns are captured in Kim Cameron's work (1991).

Cameron (1991) tries to integrate the findings of ten life-cycle models into a metamodel. Within his model are four stages: (1) entrepreneurship, (2) collectivity, (3) formalization and control, and (4) elaboration of structure. As in other models, the first stage is a time of little coordination, extensive ideas, and marshaling resources. As the organization passes into the collectivity stage, there is a greater sense of shared mission and strong commitment while innovation continues. However, during the formalization and control stage, rules and stable structures are put in place, innovation is rare, and procedures and efficiency are the foci. As the organization enters the elaboration-of-structure stage, it begins to go through a series of renewals through decentralization, expansion, or other adaptation.

Weick's social psychology of change theory reflects the life-cycle assumptions (Levy and Merry, 1986). The three stages in the model are enactment, selection, and retention. Organizations constantly cycle through these phases, in which participants select changes and make choices about retention. Retention is based on the life cycle of the organization. These short-term actions contribute to an evolutionary process in which practices, structures, and ideas change. The distinctive characteristic of this life-cycle model is that change is described as commonplace across different stages—enactment, selection, and retention happen among all employees within all life cycles, but with some distinctions in the process (Van de Ven and Poole, 1995).

The human resource tradition in companies reflects the life-cycle model as well (Bolman and Deal, 1991). Developmental theories examine human motivation, individual and group interaction, retraining, and development as central to organizational processes and change. Although human resource theories enjoy a long tradition, Bolman and Deal popularized this approach to analyzing organizations with their notion of the human resource lens. Seen through the human resource lens, organizational change is difficult for individuals because they have to change their current approach, which is tied to their identity and strengths. In order to help assuage this fear, leaders need to make the change understandable and train people to operate differently.

Key activities and individuals: This model differs from both of the earlier models in that it begins to emphasize people throughout the organization as critical to the change process. Change will not occur successfully unless all people are prepared for it. This model shifts emphasis from the leaders or a few internal characteristics to activities throughout the organization. Each individual plays a critical role in adjusting to the life cycle. Activities focus on individual development, overcoming fear of change, training, and development. Leaders analyze the need for training, assess the institutional culture, and monitor the environment and life cycle.

As leaders determine the life cycle or development of the organization, they work with people based on the principles of each stage. Young organizations need creativity and entrepreneurship through marshaling resources and creating an ideology. As the organization evolves to the mature stage, it needs to focus on internal processes and practices rather than external factors. Over time, renewal and expansion occur through managers observing the environment and selectively responding.

Benefits and criticisms: The benefit of these models is that they focus on a previously missing aspect of change: the fact that organizations proceed through different phases. Most earlier models treated organizations as differing in type according to sector, size, and so forth, but not in terms of development.

Focusing on change over time has proven to be theoretically sound in many studies. Also, the focus on people throughout the organization is an important shift from focusing on leaders or the environment. Furthermore, the importance of training has proven central to many change efforts, and later models that combined assumptions from several theories adopted principles about training (Senge, 1990). Some recent teleological models, like TQM, include ongoing staff development. However, many propositions of the model have either not held up within studies or are untested, making the contributions of this category of models unknown (Burnes, 1996).

Most of the literature on life-cycle models is conceptual rather than empirical, and their efficacy is not well established. Another concern is the overly deterministic character of these models, as the nature of organizational change and its stages are somewhat predetermined. Some theorists suggest that only birth, youth, and maturity exist, and that organizational decline can be avoided (Lippitt, 1969). Also, some models suggest that managers can speed up, slow down, or even abort certain stages, suggesting more human agency and less determinism. A few studies that have examined life-cycle models have found that organizations did not proceed through the stages in the proposed sequence. Researchers have argued for the importance of the notion of stages, as it allows organizational participants to be responsive to changes and to see them as natural. Developmental models (focused on stages and the necessity of training) appear to have greater empirical support than other models in this category.

> **The name *dialectical* refers directly to the Hegelian-Marxian perspective in which a pattern, value, ideal, or norm in an organization is always present with its polar opposite.**

Dialectical

Dialectical models (Van de Ven and Poole, 1995) and the political metaphor of change (Morgan, 1986) are similar in their assumptions. The name *dialectical* refers directly to the Hegelian-Marxian perspective in which a pattern, value, ideal, or norm in an organization is always present with its polar opposite. An example in higher education institutions would be the pattern of communitarianism, with the opposing value of individualism. These two forces are always influencing each other, and over time change is created through the interaction of opposing forces. Interestingly, Czarniawska and Sevon (1996) characterized the change literature itself as a dialectical pattern in which the planned change and evolutionary models represent opposites, generating the four other typologies of models.

Assumptions: Organizations pass through long periods of evolutionary change (as the dialectical interaction between the polar opposites occurs) and short periods of second-order or revolutionary change, when there is an impasse between the two perspectives (Morgan, 1986). An organization's polar opposite belief systems eventually clash, resulting in radical change. Conflict is seen as an inherent attribute of human interaction. The outcome of change is a modified organizational ideology or identity. Predominant change processes are bargaining, consciousness-raising, persuasion, influence and power, and social movements (Bolman and Deal, 1991). Leaders are key within any social movement and are a central part of these models, yet collective action is usually the primary focus. Progress and rationality are not necessarily part of this theory of change; dialectical conflict does not necessarily produce a "better" organization.

Political or dialectical models sometimes share assumptions with cultural models. Political models examine how a dominant culture shapes (and reshapes) organizational processes; this culture is referred to as the *power culture* (Benjamin, 1996). Organizations are perceived as political entities in which dominant coalitions manipulate their power to preserve the status quo and maintain their privilege. Another way that political models overlap with cultural models is in their emphasis on social movements and subgroups or subcultures.

Dialectical models do not assume that everyone is involved; instead they emphasize that inactivity is quite prevalent (Baldridge, Curtis, Ecker, and Riley, 1977). Few people participate in governance or are strongly interested in change. People who create change can become involved in interest groups, flowing in and out. When resources are plentiful, few people worry about changes or engage in conflict. When resources are constrained and changes are pending (or an inability to create changes exists due to lack of resources), then people mobilize. These models focus on human motivation and needs; intuition is just as important as the facts and figures that are emphasized within other models (Bergquist, 1992; Lindquist, 1978). Social interaction is more critical than environmental scanning, planning, or assessing the life cycle of the organization. The metaphor is a social movement.

Examples: Early dialectical scholars studied interest groups and social movements within organizations (Levy and Merry, 1986). Later, studies took two general directions, seeing politics as negative (exploitation and dominance) or positive (creating vision and collective goals).

Kotter (1985) provides an analysis of the skills needed to create political change: (1) agenda-setting, (2) networking and forming coalitions, and (3) bargaining and negotiation. Setting an agenda is different than establishing a vision, a typical process within teleological models that is usually leader-derived. Instead, setting an agenda involves listening to people throughout the organization and including their interests; agendas are responsive to stakeholder concerns (Bolman and Deal, 1991). Networking is the next step for creating change. In order to build coalitions, change agents need to identify key people who will facilitate change as well as individuals who will resist the change. One of the primary purposes of networking is developing relationships with key people who can overcome resistance, so that they can be used to influence other people when necessary. Change agents must also develop a power base by succeeding at certain efforts and aligning themselves with other powerful individuals. Once the change agent has an agenda, a network, coalitions, and a power base, then he or she is ready to bargain and negotiate in order to create change. Bolman and Deal (1991) review several bargaining strategies that have been found effective in creating change. Empowerment approaches to change represent an even more positive spin on the political approach to creating change. In these approaches, change agents are encouraged to examine whether the change has mutually beneficial consequences for all involved parties, is moral, and demonstrates caring for employees (Bolman and Deal, 1991). A few studies have illustrated that empowerment models are instrumental in facilitating change (Astin and Leland, 1991; Bensimon and Neumann, 1993).

Marxist theory as applied to organizations has always been prevalent within this tradition. Analyses of the development of collective bargaining and labor unions within organizations tend to use a Marxist perspective. The findings of studies suggest that boards and other organizational leaders create structures that prevent equitable treatment and serve an elite's interest (Morgan, 1986; Rhoades, 1998). Change initiatives are usually developed for efficiency and cost-containment purposes that reflect the elite's interests rather than a shared interest (Morgan, 1986). There is a dialectical tension related to change and whose interests are served. Current studies about gender and ethnic diversity in organizations, and the possibility of changing structures and culture, have been interpreted through the dialectical lens. Several studies examined the need to completely restructure organizations and develop new cultures because the existing structures are embedded with patriarchal values (Calas and Smirich, 1992; Townsend and Twombly, 1998). For example, policies that prevent women's advancement—such as lack of maternity leave or restrictive criteria for promotion—create change, as the interest group determines needs and discovers conflict. The dominant patriarchal ideology is revealed, and it becomes apparent that change must occur in order to create an environment that is open to women (Calas and Smirich, 1992). These models tend to assume that evolutionary change will not be able to move organizations forward to embrace women, because evolutionary change usually does not diverge markedly from the status quo.

Key activities and individuals: Similar to the life-cycle category, this model focuses on individuals throughout the organization as part of the dialectical change process. Conflict is a result of focusing on the views of all, not just positional leaders. Although an elite or dominant ideology often tries to maintain power and authority, tension eventually builds up, leading to change. However, the model also suggests that many people will choose to be inactive in the process. Activities are not a major focus within these models. Bargaining, persuasion, and conflict are inherent aspects of human nature that do not need to be deliberately developed. This model is similar to evolutionary models in its de-emphasis of activities that should be fostered. Inherent conflict will create change; thus, this model has a deterministic nature as well. The perspectives exist and will, whether or not organizations want them to, come into conflict eventually.

Benefits and criticisms. A major benefit of these models is their departure from the focus on rationality and linearity. Evolutionary, life-cycle, and teleological models all emphasize that change is rational and progressive, leading toward something better (although not all life-cycle models assume a progressive stance). Many theorists have pointed to changes that were not for the good of organizations and have often noted the erratic, political nature of organizational change (Morgan, 1986). This model provided explanation for regressive change and highlighted irrationality. The more popular dialectical models are those that emphasize social movements and leaders' roles, providing a strong and hopeful analogy for change. People can compare their organization's change efforts to such positive events as the civil rights movement. These theories certainly do not offer a picture of moral superiority, but in popular adaptation, they are often viewed as doing so.

The deterministic nature of the model is critiqued by scholars as it has been within other models. The lack of emphasis on the environment is seen as problematic. For example, the dialectical tension is never related to any forces outside itself. Baldridge, Curtis, Ecker, and Riley (1977) note that their original political models of higher education organizations underestimated the impact of environmental influences on political processes and anticipated a stronger relationship between political processes and environmental issues. This is an area in need of future research. Also, some theorists wonder whether this tension and the polar opposite forces could not be managed (teleological) or if training could help people to exist within this tension-filled environment (life cycle). A more general criticism is that these models offer little guidance to organizations or leaders. This may be a product of the models themselves, or it may be a result of the way they have been applied.

Social Cognition

Social-cognition models have gained popularity in the last twenty years. A variety of models emphasize cognition, from sensemaking to institutionalism to imaginization (Morgan, 1986; Scott, 1995; Weick, 1995). These models tend to come from a phenomenological or social-constructivist view of organizations (hence the term *social* in combination with *cognition*), although not all of them do. The earlier typologies (teleological, evolutionary, life cycle, political) emerged from functionalist approaches to viewing organizations. Functionalists hold that there is a single organizational reality that all people generally perceive similarly.

Assumptions: Prior to the development of cognitive models, the process of learning and development had already been coupled with change through life-cycle models (Argyris, 1982). Cognitive models built on the foundation of life-cycle models by examining in greater detail how learning occurs and even tying the notion of change more directly to learning. Studies of resistance to change illustrated the need for people to learn new approaches and examined how such learning might occur. New phenomena related to cognition and change were discerned, such as knowledge structures, paradigms, schema, cybernetics, sensemaking, cognitive dissonance, cause maps, and interpretation, which are all key concepts within these theories (Bushe and Shani, 1991; March, 1991; Morgan, 1986). Research on how the brain works revealed that knowledge is usually developed by building on past information called *knowledge structures* or *schema*, prompting theorists to contemplate how proposals for institutional change could build on prior organizational knowledge (Hedberg, 1981). Learning also occurs as two pieces of conflicting information are brought together, in a phenomenon often labeled *cognitive dissonance* (Argyris, 1994). Theorists wondered how dissonance helped facilitate change.

Functionalists hold that there is a single organizational reality that all people perceive similarly.

The reasons for change in organizations are tied to appropriateness and a reaction to cognitive dissonance (Collins, 1998). There is not necessarily an environmental necessity, a developmental challenge, a leader's vision, or dialectical or ideological tension. Instead, people simply reach a point of cognitive dissonance at which values and actions clash or something seems outmoded, and they decide to change. *Cybernetics* is the term used to describe the complex approach to change within social cognition; it is an interactive model, with tensions and strains common within circular systems (Morgan, 1986). Thus, change does not occur linearly or in stages—instead it is a multifaceted, interconnected, overlapping series of processes, obstacles, and individuals. The outcome of change is a new frame of mind or worldview. The metaphor for this approach to change is usually the brain: complex, interrelated systems, mental models, and interpretation.

Social-cognition models examine how leaders shape the change process through framing and interpretation, and how individuals within the organization interpret and make sense of change (Harris, 1996). The environment cannot be objectively determined, but is interpreted by leaders. This is why the environment is seen as a lesser force, because it is socially constructed and multiple (March, 1991). Social-cognition theorists tend to be interested in how employees frame the organization or how worldviews can be shaped and changed through learning. Change can be understood and enacted only through individuals (Harris, 1996; Martin, 1992). These theories reject a shared reality or organizational culture. Part of the difficulty of creating change is realizing that people are interpreting their environment so differently. Within social-cognition models, habits, and organizational identity are examined, relating them to life-cycle theories in which organizational identity and identification are important to understand factors in resistance to change. Facilitating change is sometimes explored as the process of allowing people to let go of the identity attached to past strategies and successes (Morgan, 1986).

Examples: Argyris' single- and double-loop learning theory reflects the social-cognition perspective and is a key concept in organizational learning and change. *Single-loop learning* refers to retaining existing norms, goals, and structures and improving on current methods (Argyris, 1982, 1994). This is often associated with first-order change and an internal standard of performance such as employees' views of quality. In contrast, *double-loop learning* refers to the process by which existing norms, goals, and structures are reformulated to create innovative solutions. It is usually associated with second-order change and employs external standards of performance such as state-mandated regulations of quality. In double-loop learning, people or organizations come to terms with problems or mismatches in the governing variables (beliefs) that guide their actions (Hedberg, 1981). The common assumption that people are driven to fix inconsistencies between their thoughts and actions or between their actions and consequences was shown to be invalid. An environment of trust must be created in order to have double-loop learning, as people on their own will not challenge or examine inconsistencies (Argyris, 1982).

In addition, organizational change is seen as a learning process affected by organizational and environmental conditions and by theories of action held by the organization's members (March, 1991). Theories of action are the views that people hold, even if they do not act on such views. The important principle for organizational change is that people may describe that they have initiated a change or believe in a change, but may not enact that change. Organizations need to identify the social-cognition approach of employees—their theories of action—and align them with espoused organizational values and change initiatives. Research on misalignment between espoused and enacted theories led to models of paradigm-shifting.

Models of paradigm-shifting and future-envisioning focus on identifying the views or beliefs of organizational participants (through operational presuppositions and scanning the environment), then providing leaders with training on how to lead people to conceptualize a different organizational reality (Levy and Merry, 1986). Some models focus on helping members cope with the loss and death of the old organizational paradigm. Future-envisioning focuses organizational members' attention on the desired future, rather than on the present situation and organization.

The emphasis on different paradigms or ways of viewing the organization spawned work by researchers such as Cohen and March (1991a, 1991b); Bolman and Deal (1991); Morgan (1986); and Weick (1995), examining organizations through a social-constructivist perspective, in which it is acknowledged that there are multiple views of organizational reality. These theorists suggest that change can be accomplished by leaders who view the organization through different lenses, examining issues through the logic of perspectives. Bolman and Deal (1991) suggest that leaders need to see change as a structural issue though the bureaucratic lens; as a training issue, through the human resource lens; as a power issue, through the political lens; and as an issue of identity and meaning, through the symbolic lens. Leaders create change by helping employees to view the organization through different lenses and by reframing issues so that different people can understand and enact the needed change.

Sensemaking is another example of this category and emerged from the focus on paradigms, cognition, and multiple realities (Weick, 1995). It emphasizes how people interpret their world and reconstruct reality on an ongoing basis. Constructing this reality is an effort to create order and make retrospective sense out of what happens. Sensemaking focuses on how worldviews are shaped and altered. But there is a strong contextual rationality (the sense made is appropriate to the context) and a focus on intersubjective meaning (individuals' perspectives). Weick distinguishes sensemaking from interpretation; sensemaking is about how people generate that which they interpret (Weick, 1995, p. 13). Change situations may evoke sensemaking by altering the order that people have created. Weick emphasizes the roles of wisdom, acceptance of a high level of ignorance, and learning and resilience within organizations as facilitators of change (Weick, 1993). Learning, humility, resilience, and wisdom help enable individuals to alter their current reality.

Key activities and individuals: These models are similar to dialectical models in their emphasis on individuals throughout the organizations as key to understanding and facilitating change. In fact, these models are broader in scope, paying more attention to each individual as constructing reality uniquely. Dialectical approaches tend to conceptualize people as having group interests and perspectives, rather than individual ones. Change activities focused on within social cognition are learning, schema development, altering beliefs, and aligning the individual's identity/worldview and actions. Leaders assess situations through different lenses, then help reframe worldviews through the use of metaphors or models so that different people can understand the change (Morgan, 1986).

Morgan (1986) presents the example of an organization facing a change initiative through the social-cognition model: leaders would analyze the situation through the political perspective, then the evolutionary perspective, then the life-cycle perspective. These various worldviews provide different evidence about how to approach the change; the process is then aligned with the model that best suits the situation. Leaders also alter shared norms and understandings, help individuals shift paradigms, or create an environment of trust so double-loop learning can occur.

Benefits and Criticisms: One of the major contributions of these theories is a more phenomenological approach to the study of change, vastly expanding the interpersonal and human aspects of change. Individual meaning construction was mostly left out of theories that focused on systems, organizational dialectical tension, the environment, the life cycles of organizations, or scientific management structures. These other perspectives discount the individuals that make up the system; change is, after all, about individual learning and sensemaking. The realization that change often fails because individuals simply do not understand or comprehend the change at hand has been helpful, particularly to those within the teleological framework. This provides managers with new tools for creating and leading change.

Also, similar to dialectical models, social-cognition models illustrate that change is not always progressive or positive. For example, institutions that serve an important purpose and evolve to another, less important role are not necessarily progressing. Social-cognition models examine *how* change occurs (through learning, for example), rather than just identifying variables associated with change, the latter approach being common within evolutionary and teleological models (such variables may include senior management vision, political environment, new institutional structure, or orientation toward effectiveness). This provided needed nuanced data at a more micro level of the organization.

One criticism of social-cognition models has been that they de-emphasize the effects of environment and external forces on change. The systemic view and interconnected nature is sometimes lost when a focus on individuals and their perceptions is adopted. Some models within this perspective have tried to incorporate the environment, examining how individuals interpret the environment or system. Yet the underlying assumption is that there is no such independent system, beyond individuals. Also, some models suggest that individuals are pliable (Bolman and Deal, 1991; Morgan, 1996); this is also noted as a problem within teleological models. Some writers focus on changing people's realities and worldviews (Nevis, Lancourt, and Vassallo, 1996). Critics claim that these models overemphasize people's ability to change such fundamental aspects of their identity and reality. A direct criticism from cultural models is that social cognition ignores values, feelings, and emotions for the most part. Its emphasis on thinking, mental processes, and learning tends to exclude other aspects in understanding the nature of change, how it occurs, and why it occurs.

Cultural

Most models of change describe organizations as rational places with norms and rules. The major contribution of cultural models to the change literature is their emphasis on irrationality (also emphasized in dialectical models), the spirit or unconscious, and the fluidity and complexity of organizations (also noted in social cognition). Cultural models blend the assumptions of the social-cognition and dialectical methods.

Cultural models blend the assumptions of the social-cognition and dialectical methods.

Assumptions: Change occurs naturally as a response to alterations in the human environment; cultures are always changing (Morgan, 1986). Cultural and dialectical models often overlap with the image of social movements as an analogy for cultural and political change (Morgan, 1986). The change process tends to be long-term and slow. Change within an organization entails alteration of values, beliefs, myths, and rituals (Schein, 1985). There is an emphasis on the symbolic nature of organizations, rather than the structural, human, or cognitive aspects emphasized within earlier theories. History and traditions are important to understand, as they represent the collection of change processes over time. Cultural approaches share many assumptions with social-cognition theories; change can be planned or unplanned, can be regressive or progressive, and can contain intended or unintended outcomes and actions (Smirich, 1983). Change tends to be nonlinear, irrational, nonpredictable, ongoing, and dynamic (Smirich, 1983). Some cultural models focus on the leaders' ability to translate the change to individuals throughout the organizations through the use of symbolic actions, language, or metaphors as the key to creating change (Feldman, 1991). If there is an external motivator, it tends to be legitimacy, which is the primary motivator within the cultural model, rather than profit or productivity, which exemplify the teleological and environmental models.

Cultural approaches tend to emphasize phenomenological and social-constructivist approaches to the study of organizations. They also suggest the difficulty of deep change, realizing that radical change involves core modifications that are unlikely to occur without alterations of fundamental beliefs. One only needs to look at the research on cultural change within history, anthropology, or political science to realize that such change is often long-term, nonsequential, and seemingly unmanageable.

Examples: The earliest types of models within this category were paradigm-shifting and future-envisioning. Early models attempted to move away from the static view of organizations provided within teleological models such as organizational development and to examine fluid, dynamic, and complex processes that shape change, such as unconsciousness, energy, spirit, mission, purpose, belief systems, myths, worldview, symbols, and state of being. Some cultural theories purport to create change managers who understand the symbolic nature of organizations; Rosabeth Kanter's famous book, *The Change Masters* (1983), epitomizes this tradition. Paradigm-shifting originally represented a cultural approach and social-cognition model, but over time, the rational management techniques that became associated with it have made many scholars identify these models as part of the teleological tradition. However, models of changing consciousness and rechanneling energy, which focus on spirit and the symbolic and deeper realities of organizations, remain embedded within the cultural perspective. An example of these approaches is the formation of consciousness groups within organizations. These groups meet and discuss the organizational identity and values, how people fit with or relate to the institutional identity, and ways that the values and identity are expressed, and delve into implicit and explicit values and basic assumptions. The purpose of such discussion is to understand the culture at a deeper level in order to foster change.

Schein (1985) is perhaps one of the best-known theorists of cultural change. Culture is a collective and shared phenomenon; it is reflected at different levels through the organizational mission, through individual beliefs, and subconsciously. Change occurs as various aspects of the organizational culture are altered; for example, if the mission is realigned or new rituals or myths are developed. His perspective on culture is reflected in the symbolic action approach, in which managers create change by modifying organizational member's shared meaning—in other words, leaders re-create aspects of the symbolic system and culture. For example, leaders interpret events and history for people and create ceremonies and events that alter culture, thereby creating change (Cameron, 1991). Schein believes that certain cultures can be developed that are more open or prone to change.

Dawson illustrates a very different cultural approach in the processual change model. He studied change contextually, over time, examining the interconnection of substance, contexts, and politics (Dawson, 1994). The study developed fifteen principles for change, such as ensuring that change strategies are culturally sensitive and appreciate the potential tenacity of existing cultures; the need to fully understand and communicate the substance of change, because delay and conflict will otherwise emerge; and the fact that transition is unlikely to be marked by a line of continual improvement from beginning to end.

Interpretive strategy is another example of a cultural model, based on the assumptions that reality is socially constructed and the organization is a collection of cooperative social agreements in which individuals strive for the good of the overall organization (Chaffee, 1983). This approach entails developing orienting metaphors in order to lead or guide individuals' attitudes, altering the metaphors and thereby creating change. People are guided by metaphors that relate to important organizational aspects that have meaning for them, such as the history of the institution, rituals, or relationships with key individuals. The language associated with these metaphors reflects how the organization interacts with the external environment. It is difficult to develop a specific approach for this strategy, as it depends on the particular context (Chaffee, 1983). Context tends to be critical across all models. Interpretive strategy stresses that reality is incoherent, attitudinal, and cognitively complex; change must be organizationwide, not just among top management; and motivation is more critical than information from environmental scanning or institutional assessment.

Key activities or individuals: Cultural theories, like social-cognition models, tend to emphasize the collective process of change and the key role of each individual. The most popular cultural models focus on leaders' ability to shape organizational culture and on culture as collective or shared. Some cultural theories focus on all organizational participants as unique in their interpretation of organizational culture and illustrate the difficulty of creating change (Martin, 1992). The key activities to create change include modifying the mission and vision, creating new myths and rituals, leaders performing symbolic actions, using metaphors, assessing the institutional culture, tapping into energy, developing enthusiasm, altering motivations of people through spirituality, and communicating values and beliefs.

Benefits and criticisms: The emphasis on context, complexity, and contradiction is an important contribution of cultural scholars (Collins, 1998). The focus on values and beliefs within cultural models had been mostly overlooked by many theories. More recent social-cognition theories have incorporated and broadened their view to include the full range of human behavior, following the lead of cultural theories. Also, this set of theories reemphasized the temporal dimension of change (especially the extremely lengthy process related to second-order change) which was not emphasized in social-cognition and teleological models that had gained popularity over evolutionary and dialectical models in recent years (Collins, 1998). Revealing the relationship between institutional culture and change is also a major contribution. The promise of the emphasis on spirituality and unconscious processes has not really been investigated or illustrated at this point.

Models such as Schein's (1985), in which culture is seen simplistically as a collective and shared process among all organizational members and one that can be manipulated and managed, have come under serious criticism for oversimplifying the notion of culture. The assumption of plasticity of people, noted as problematic in the section on teleological models, is also voiced about theories of "managing culture" or "creating a culture of change" (Collins, 1998). More complex models of culture have evolved, but have been criticized for other reasons. For example, Burnes (1996) notes that a cultural perspective is often perceived as problematic because change is conceptualized as being so long-term and the layers of culture are so complex. Thus, this perspective is sometimes seen as impractical for application.

Multiple Models

Some researchers suggest using an amalgam of several models or categories, as each sheds light on different aspects of organizational life (Van de Ven and Poole, 1995). The advantage to multiple models is that they combine the insights of various change theories. Several examples of multiple models are presented to illustrate how assumptions from teleological, evolutionary, political, cultural, social-cognition, and life-cycle models can be combined to understand change. For example, Morgan (1986) suggests that a combination of evolutionary, dialectical, and cognitive theories best represents change within organizations. Rajagopalan and Spreitzer (1996) combined cognitive, evolutionary (rational), and scientific management (learning) theories into a model of strategic change for businesses, exploiting the theoretical synergy of the models. Rajagopalan and Spreitzer argue that the perspectives are not irreconcilable, as others have critiqued. They note, for instance, that scientific management theories correct the weakness of evolutionary theories that exclude managerial actions. Each theory is seen as counteracting a weakness within the other.

One popular example of multiple models is Bolman and Deal's four frames of organizational change (1991). They note that the different organizational theories also represent unique ways people approach or act in organizations, and that by combining the various theories or lenses, leaders can more accurately assess situations and move toward solutions (Bolman and Deal, 1991). Multidimensional thinking is identified as characterizing the best and most successful managers. The four lenses examined are: human resource, structural, political, and symbolic. For example, through a symbolic lens, leaders can see how change results in a loss of meaning and purpose—people form attachments to symbols and have difficulty letting go. Through a political perspective, change generates conflict; managing change effectively requires the creation of arenas in which issues can be negotiated. Change also alters stable roles and relationships, creating confusion. Attention to structure through the realignment of formal patterns and policies helps to facilitate change. Last, people can feel incompetent, needy, or powerless as a result of change. Psychological support can be provided through training and opportunities for involvement (Bolman and Deal, 1991). It is the leader's role to provide all these aspects.

Senge's model of learning organizations (1990) blends evolutionary, social-cognition, cultural, and teleological models, even though it is mostly a reflection of teleological assumptions. Learning organizations characterize managers as using systems, thinking to create change by examining interrelationships that shape system behavior, and acting in tune with larger natural and economic processes (notice the similarity to evolutionary assumptions). He also notes the importance of examining our mental models in order to foster change. Managers are to reflect, clarify, and improve the internal pictures of the world and notice how they shape actions (also described by Bolman and Deal, 1991; Morgan, 1986). A cultural approach is exemplified by the need to create a culture in which all members develop so that they can achieve their goals and purposes, ideally aligned with institutional change efforts. Life-cycle models are reflected, to some degree, through the emphasis on human development. Last, the model illustrates teleological assumptions about the manager as the active force that enacts the core disciplines of a learning organization: (1) developing your personal mastery (personal vision, holding creative tension, commitment to truth, and the like); (2) identifying and altering mental models; (3) creating shared vision; (4) systems thinking; and (5) fostering team learning. The emphasis on vision, working in teams, and the leader creating a shared vision for the organization reflects the teleological tradition. This may account for the popularity of Senge's model: it responds to the research on change, incorporating many of the key principles that we know, but takes a teleological approach and provides organizations with a rational model that managers can enact.

Another well-known model is Pettigrew's open learning system (1985). The scholar describes environmental assessment and strategy as critical, but also believes that leaders are central, operational changes need realigning, and human resources need to be developed for change to be successfully executed (Burnes, 1996; Pettigrew, 1985). As noted in the beginning of this article, evolutionary and teleological approaches are the most commonly combined because the two approaches keep critiquing and correcting each other.

Others researchers use the various models as a way to examine different aspects or levels of the change process. For example, Burnes (1996) notes how evolutionary or contingency models can be used for examining change at the broadest level, life-cycle models can be used to determine the life stage of the organization, cultural models might reveal the intricacies of the organizations power and interest groups, and social-cognition theories can be used to analyze individual worldviews. This seems to be a powerful perspective that few researchers have adopted.

Summary

This article has reviewed the six major categories of change models or theories, focusing on their assumptions, examples, key activities and individuals, benefits, and possible weaknesses. The life-cycle, evolutionary, and teleological models have all been critiqued for emphasizing stages (for example, growth or phases of strategy) and linearity. The political and social-cognition theories have been touted for their sophistication in illustrating complexity and in showing the regressive phases of change, ambiguity, struggle, and sometimes irrationality. Yet political and social-cognition models generally ignore the environment or system and have limited ability to predict change. Cultural models embrace a more systematic view and reveal the complications of second order-change, but often provide limited practical advice or tools. Each model appears to suffer from some interpretive weakness and to have some strengths in furthering our understanding. As we move into the application of these models within higher education, it is important to focus on both the strengths and weaknesses of these models. After reviewing these six models of organizational change, I have concluded that the strongest approach is to combine certain assumptions from various approaches. This monograph will examine the application of these theories to higher education. However, first it is important to describe the distinctive features of higher education, which is the focus of the next article. The reason for providing this analysis is to develop an approach to change that is sensitive to higher education's distinctive character in order to apply these theories contextually, as cultural models have suggested is crucial.

APPENDIX 1

	Evolutionary	Teleological	Life Cycle	Political	Social Cognition	Cultural
Why change occurs	External environment	Leaders; internal environment	Leaders guiding individual's natural growth	Dialectical tension of values, norms, or patterns	Cognitive dissonance; appropriateness	Response to alterations in the human environment
Process of change	Adaption; slow; gradual; non-intentional	Rational; linear; purposeful	Natural progression; result of training and motivation; altering habits and identity	First order followed by occasional second order; negotiation and power	Learning; altering paradigms or lens; interconnected and complex	Long-term; slow; symbolic process; nonlinear; unpredicatble
Outcomes of change	New structures and processes; first order	New structures and organizing principles	New organizational identity	New organizational ideology	New frame of mind	New culture
Key metaphor	Self-producing organism	Changemaster	Teacher	Social movement	Brain	Social movement
Examples	Resource dependency; strategic choice; population ecology	Organizational development, strategic planning; reengineering; TQM	Developmental models; organizational decline; social psychology of change	Empowerment; bargaining; political change; Marxist theory	Single- and double-looped learning; paradigm-shifting; sensemaking	Interpretive strategy; paradigm-shifting; processual change

(continued)

APPENDIX 1 (*Continued*)

	Evolutionary	Teleological	Life Cycle	Political	Social Cognition	Cultural
Criticisms	Lack of human emphasis; deterministic quality	Overly rational and linear; inability to explain second-order change; plasticity of people	Little empirical proof; deterministic character	Deterministic; lack of environmental concerns; little guidance for leaders	Deemphasizes environment; overemphasizes ease of change; ignores values and emotions;	Impractical to guide leaders; focus on universalistic culture; mostly untested
Benefits	Environmental emphasis; systems approach	Importance of change agents; management techniques and strategies	Change related to phases; temporal aspect; focus on people throughout the organization	Change not always progressive; irrationality; role of power	Emphasizes socially constructed nature; emphasis on individuals; habits and attitudes as barriers	Context; Irrationality; values, and beliefs; complexity; multiple levels of change

Understanding the Nature of Higher Education Organizations: Key to Successful Organizational Change

GORDON WINSTON asks a compelling question in his article, *Creating a Context for Change*: "Why can't a college be more like a firm?" (Winston, 1998, p. 52). He notes the current urgency and need for change, and fears that higher education's unique context will cause it to lag behind the many changes occurring in corporate America. Winston answers his own question by suggesting that higher education is a unique industry and needs to be conscious about this distinctiveness as it engages organizational change. This monograph maintains Winston's assumption that higher education needs to develop its own change concepts, methodology, and language rooted in its value system and culture. To honor this assumption, I synthesize what we know about the unique environment of higher education and examine the implications for change in that context. There are two main reasons this is necessary for developing a distinctive approach to higher education: (1) overlooking these factors may result in mistakes in analysis and strategy, and (2) using concepts foreign to the values of the academy will most likely fail to engage people who must bring about the change.

Some commentators worry that if higher education develops its own approach to change that is aligned with its values system, legislatures and the general public, focused on efficiency and corporate change analogies, will not understand or appreciate the academy's perspective (Green, 1998). Nonetheless, I echo MacDonald's call for measured change (1997) rather than the wholesale change advocated in popular rhetoric by management consultants and now among legislatures. Higher education, as a long-standing institution, needs to approach change in a cautious way that takes into account its structure and values system. This measured approach to change is also described within the literature on nonprofit organizations and professional bureaucracies such as those of lawyers, accountants, or doctors (Drucker, 1990; Handy, 1994, 1995; Wheatley, 1999). Therefore, this situation is not unique to higher education; other professions and organizations are developing distinctive change models to fit their contexts.

Some interesting research on change within the nonprofit sector will serve to frame this discussion on the unique environment of higher education, but the reader is also encouraged to research professional bureaucracies that face the same challenge as higher education institutions. Critiques of change models from the nonprofit sector note that society's interest in reliable institutions and nonprofits' missions, with a consistent value system, makes the assumptions of many evolutionary change models mostly irrelevant (Salipante and Golden-Biddle, 1995). In general, continuity has been identified as a critical factor within the change models of nonprofit organizations. Change and continuity should be seen hand-in-hand; change can threaten an organization's core mission, expertise, and basic character and identity. Responding to external environments has threatened the livelihood of some nonprofits. Furthermore, reacting to the calls for change by one generation of society can create chaos for organizations. The mission of the nonprofit institution may not be served by changing to meet ephemeral societal change.

Other problematic assumptions within evolutionary, scientific management (teleological), and life-cycle models are pointed out in these studies. External environments are shown to be socially constructed and lacking a logic of their own. Organizational members are not rational, flexible, and subservient (Salipante and Golden-Biddle, 1995). Nonprofits were unsuccessful when leaders scrutinized environmental challenges and made adjustments to staff and structure. Additionally, newer biological theories suggest that many living systems are closed, not open, as previously understood (Morgan, 1986, p. 236). Instead, systems are more self-contained and change is less reflective of external forces than was previously conceptualized. Studies of nonprofit institutions have shown that maintaining a stable pattern of relationships is important for survival and tends to lead to growth and renewal. They also determined that unlike businesses, nonprofit institutions are less likely to pass through stages of maturation; instead they are stable institutions exhibiting limited or no development or stages (Salipante and Golden-Biddle, 1995). Cultural and social-cognition models were found to be most insightful for explaining the change process in nonprofit organizations. These unique institutional characteristics, such as long-standing social mission, also characterize higher education institutions. A similar pattern is likely to be found as these theories are applied to higher education institutions.

This article is organized based on the distinctive features of higher education institutions identified in the research: (1) interdependent organization, (2) relatively independent of environment, (3) unique culture of the academy, (4) institutional status, (5) values-driven, (6) multiple power and authority structures, (7) loosely coupled system, (8) organized anarchical decision-making, (9) professional and administrative values, (10) shared governance, (11) employee commitment and tenure, (12) goal ambiguity, and (13) image and success. Although not an exhaustive list, this represents some of the key features of higher education institutions that influence organizational change. For an even more detailed description of these various features, see Bergquist, 1992; Birnbaum, 1991a; Clark, 1983a; Sporn, 1999. There will be some overlap in the discussion—for example, loosely coupled systems result in organized anarchical decision-making, and the professional and administrative values distinction reflects the unique power and authority structures. The occasional overlap will help to further illustrate that these characteristics define the very nature of these institutions and are deeply embedded within the structure and culture. The reader also needs to be aware that these distinctive characteristics vary by institutional type. The different ways that characteristics such as goal ambiguity or image emerge within community colleges or research universities will be noted within each section.

This article also describes several current trends that are affecting the distinctive features of higher education institutions, such as the massive retirement of faculty (close to 40 percent) in the next decade; growth of part-time and contract faculty; new accountability structures such as performance funding; growing emphasis on collaboration, increased pressures from the external environment; diversification of faculty, staff; and students; and disintegration of shared governance (Kezar, 2000a). In addition to noting some current trends related to these distinctive characteristics, I will also make some observations about the ways that these characteristics may influence the change process in higher education. These observations are not based on research, but are arguments derived from critical analysis of the literature. Last, it should be noted that this article does not reflect the characteristics of for-profit higher education institutions that tend to operate more similarly to business organizations.

Interdependent Organizations

Some higher education scholars have noted that universities do not operate independently of disciplinary societies, the federal government, and other significant forces. Alpert, for example, suggests that higher education institutions need to realize that they are not fully autonomous and cannot set a course of action independent of other institutions (1991). He provides the example of "a research university in which 10,000 departments exist that are arrayed in about 100 disciplinary communities on about 100 major research campuses and tied together in an interdependent national system" (Alpert, 1991, p. 87). Disciplinary societies and communities extend across institutional boundaries and have, since their origin, shaped changes on individual college campuses. Alpert did not describe accreditation agencies that also have disciplinary connections, associations such as the American Council on Education or American Association for Higher Education, unions, and private foundations. These represent other parts of this interdependent system, which Bob Berdhal (1991) has called the ecology of higher education.

Accreditation evolved in order to change higher education institutions, to make them more standardized and of higher quality (Berdhal, 1991; Cohen, 1998; Costello, 1994). In addition, one of the primary roles of accreditation has been improvement of higher education. Although accountability and standards have been the overriding goals, especially within the past few decades, these regional organizations have emphasized faculty roles, diversity, outcomes assessment, and other changes they feel are necessary (Kezar and El-Khawas, forthcoming). After the turn of the last century, higher education associations developed with the purpose of providing a national perspective on trends and to lead change (Green, 2000). Foundations have long supported change agendas through grants and funding research to improve higher education. These unique parts of the higher education system are often overlooked as forces or sources of institutional change or as part of the process.

Conceptualizations such as Alpert's, which illustrate the vast complexity of higher education institutions, have led people to be concerned about whether change can be enacted in ways described within the teleological models, where managers have control and ability to guide the direction of organizations. Current trends make this web of interdependent relationships only more complex with the growth of unionization and recent revival of accreditation. The accreditation process has been altered, placing more importance on improvement than on compliance (Kezar and El-Khawas, forthcoming). While higher education institutions may be interdependent and rely heavily on outside organizations, they are relatively independent of the environment.

The interdependent nature of higher education will most likely result in institutions receiving multiple and perhaps mixed messages related to change. Change will more likely occur in areas where several forces overlap. For example, community-service learning has become widespread in the last decade because disciplinary societies, the federal government (through Americorp), presidential associations such as Campus Compact, foundations such as Kellogg, and professional associations such as the American Association for Higher Education were all recommending and reinforcing this initiative.

> **The interdependent nature of higher education will most likely result in institutions receiving multiple and perhaps mixed messages related to change.**

Relatively Independent of Environment

In terms of environmental vulnerability, higher education institutions have been noted as being in the middle of the continuum (Alpert, 1991; Berdhal, 1991; Birnbaum, 1991a). Businesses are more independent, with few regulations and a great degree of autonomy (excepting market forces). Public school districts would be farther over on the continuum, representing a captured organization with heavy regulation and subject to local, state, and federal forces to which it is extremely vulnerable. Colleges and universities vary to the degree to which they are insulated from market, social, economic, or political forces (Berdhal, 1991). Higher education has a history of a great degree of autonomy because no national ministry of higher education evolved and states have a tradition of allowing higher education its independence, with minimal local expectations (Cohen, 1998). This fluctuates over time, and there have been periods during which higher education responded to social and political needs—for example, during the world wars. In terms of change, this relative independence might suggest that environmental aspects will be less significant in the change process. However, different institutional types experience greater and lesser degrees of environmental independence. Private institutions, for example, experience greater vulnerability to market forces, whereas public institutions tend be affected by state legislatures. Thus, campuses experience different environmental forces to varying degrees, with private institutions considered to be more vulnerable.

Currently, there is great pressure for higher education to meet external demands and needs for transforming the public schools, solving social problems, and assisting local and state economic development, among other forces (Kezar, 2000a). Berdhal (1991) notes that since World War II, pieces of autonomy have been lost here and there on the road toward a system of mass access to higher education. But historical influences have created structures and cultures that are relatively autonomous. For many higher education professionals, external pressures may seem overwhelming relative to those of earlier time periods, yet higher education experiences much less scrutiny and more freedom than many enterprises. It is important to watch trends toward more environmental vulnerability, especially as market forces drive a move to a for-profit model of business, and to anticipate how they might affect the need for or approach to change.

As external pressures grow and funding is constrained, higher education institutions will be more likely to respond to external changes than they would have been in previous times, especially if there are monetary incentives related to the initiative. Thus, evolutionary models may be increasing in importance even if they have not been seen as critical to the change process in the past. However, external forces, as noted in the section on the interdependent nature of organizations, can often diffuse themselves by lacking synergy with other organizations or by canceling each other out. For example, market forces and traditional academic values appear to be operating to balance each other.

Unique Organizational Cultures of the Academy

The enterprise of higher education has been characterized as being different from other organizations in the emergence of distinctive cultures that characterize the enterprise. Article two described Bolman and Deal's four organizational cultures or frames: human resources, structural, symbolic, and political, which were found in business organizations (1991). Robert Birnbaum (1991a) and William Bergquist (1992) examined the cultures that exist within higher education institutions to see if they are distinct from those in businesses. Birnbaum found that higher education cultures were characterized as being a collegium, political system, form of organized anarchy, or bureaucracy (1991a). The collegium and organized anarchy were distinct from the cultures found by Bolman and Deal, emphasizing higher education's more consensus-based environment and less rational, organized, or clear structure. It should be noted that the collegium does overlap with Bolman and Deal's human resource frame in the importance of people within organizations, and the organized anarchy does share some characteristics with the symbolic frame in terms of ambiguity and importance of individual meaning development. However, Birnbaum (1991a) illustrates that these cultures emerge uniquely in higher education.

Bergquist identified four cultures: collegial, managerial, developmental, and negotiating. Organized anarchy was not represented as widespread in the institutions studied, and the developmental culture emerged. The collegial culture finds meaning primarily through the disciplines represented by the faculty; a quasipolitical governance processes; research and teaching; and the generation, interpretation, and dissemination of knowledge. Similar to Birnbaum's bureaucratic culture, the managerial culture finds meaning primarily in the organizational implementation and evaluation of work directed toward specific goals and purposes. The developmental culture finds meaning through the creation of programs and activities furthering the personal and professional growth of all members of the collegiate environment (essentially,

Bolman and Deal's human resources lens). Last, the negotiating culture (mostly identical to Birnbaum's political culture) finds meaning primarily in the establishment of equitable and egalitarian policies and procedures for the distribution of resources and benefits in the institution (Bergquist, 1992).

In studies that have applied these models, the collegium was found to be the most prevalent model (Smart and St. John, 1996). In addition, the political lens is more prevalent than in other sectors such as business or nonprofit, again marking a distinction in this enterprise's structure and culture. The political nature of higher education can be seen within the many subgroups that work autonomously, yet depend on one another for power and influence. Another noteworthy aspect of the unique cultures is that each institutional type reflects different combinations of cultures (Birnbaum, 1991a). Community colleges tend to be more bureaucratic, while liberal arts colleges tend to be more collegial (Bergquist, 1992).

Although there is some disagreement over the exact character or nature of the academic culture, it is clearly political yet consensus-oriented. Faculty professional values (collegium) and administrative values (bureaucratic) are both present, there is a fair degree of clashing of different value sets (political), and ambiguity and unclear structures exist (anarchical). In terms of change, the collegial orientation of higher education would suggest that a shared and inclusive process will likely be successful. In addition, political approaches are likely to be prevalent.

Several commentators have suggested that higher education institutions are becoming more entrepreneurial and market-driven as a result of technological advances, distance education, and cost constraints. Although there has not been clear empirical evidence to support this trend, it might have an impact on the culture over time (Kezar, 2000a). In addition, the growing concern about accountability among legislatures and the public might affect the varying culture of institutions.

Institutional Status

Higher education is a distinctive form of organization called an *institution*. Some of the defining characteristic of institutions are that they serve long-standing missions; are closely tied to ongoing societal needs; have set norms and socialization processes based on the mission and needs of society; and have norms that are tied closely to individuals' identities (Czarniawska and Sevon, 1996). Because these organizations have long-standing missions, they are less likely to change—and if change occurs, it is likely to happen as a result of extensive debate among stakeholders, as these organizations serve so many different societal needs. Examples of other types of organizations that are institutions include hospitals, law firms, political parties, and schools. The reason the nonprofit sector was described at the beginning of this article is that some scholars believe this sector has "institutional status" and should be treated differently from business and industry, which are more directly affected by market demands. The institutional status of higher education would suggest that change is more likely to follow the principles outlined in social-cognition models, such as the need for long-term, sustained change initiatives that work to alter individuals' mental models. Organizational habits, structures, and norms will most likely need to be reexamined.

Recent forces appear to be shaking the foundation of higher education's institutional status. Like health care, legislatures and the public are examining the question of whether higher education should remain the traditional institution that it has been. Some legislatures would like higher education to operate within the for-profit model and to abandon long-standing missions and traditions.

Values-Driven: Complex and Contrasting

Several commentators on the higher education system have noted that it is strongly values-driven (Birnbaum, 1991; Clark, 1983). Although all organizations have belief systems that guide them, colleges and universities are noted for the complex and contrasting beliefs system that guide and shape their culture and structures (Clark, 1983a, 1983b). Some values and beliefs tend to be shared across the enterprise, such as the importance of research, integrity in research, freedom to teach what is considered appropriate, the significance of shared governance and academic freedom, the belief in access to higher education, the value in specialization (this value is being dismantled since Clark documented it), and so forth, but generally there are distinctive values. For example, each disciplinary culture has distinctive beliefs and is socialized to its particular profession: mathematicians stress logic and consistency of numbers, while art historians stress perspective and interpretation. Faculty and administrators hold vastly different values sets (described in detail in a separate section. Students bring sets of beliefs and values with them to the college that often differ from those held by faculty and administrators. Clark notes that "on the basis of disciplinary subculture alone, those in academia will go on having an ever harder time understanding and identifying with one another" (1983a, p. 102). For the most part, particular roles or positions within the institution shape beliefs. The emphasis on values suggests that cultural models of change will be key to understanding and facilitating change within higher education.

This trend toward fewer shared values will become increasingly complex as individuals from diverse backgrounds enter the professoriate and join the ranks of administration and faculty. Many studies have illustrated that women, minorities, and other historically marginalized groups who have different backgrounds bring different values to their work (Astin and Leland, 1991; Calas and Smirich, 1992; Kezar, 2000a). This great differentiation in values within the institution suggests that change will be slow and difficult, and perhaps a political process in which different values systems represent different interest groups.

Multiple Power and Authority Structures

Birnbaum (1991a) noted that normative organizations such as colleges and universities rely on referent and expert power rather than coercive (prisons), reward, or legitimate power (businesses). Although power has been defined in multiple ways, in general, it is viewed as the ability of a group or person to influence or exercise control over others (Birnbaum, 1991a). Referent power results from the willingness to be influenced by another because of one's identification with them, while expert power is reflected when one person allows themselves to be influenced because the other person apparently has some special knowledge. In particular, faculty are likely to be influenced by referent power through other members of their community whom they trust, colleagues who share values with them, or appeals to principles such as ethics, rather than salary increases or administrative sanctions (Birnbaum, 1991a). In addition, autonomous faculty are unlikely to be influenced by other means of administrative influence and power, such as control or strategy. In general, power within these institutions is partially masked or secret, because in a collegial setting, it is socially unacceptable to exert power (Birnbaum, 1991a). It may take months, even years, for a new employee to determine who possesses power on campus. This would not be true among bureaucratic organizations, in which power and authority are more clearly established.

It is not just that academic institutions have unique power structures; they also have competing authority structures. Authority is the right of a person or office in an organization to demand action of others and expect those demands to be met (Birnbaum, 1991a, 1991b). Burton Clark identified four kinds of competing authority systems: academic authority, enterprise-based authority, system-based authority, and charisma (Clark, 1991a). Academic authority is maintained by the faculty and is vested in various subgroups such as disciplinary societies, associations, and collective bargaining units, all with varying power. As already noted, academic authority tends to be based in expert power. In contrast, enterprise-based authority, which includes trustees or other institutional authorities, is the legal right to act on behalf of the institution. It is essentially a position-based authority. Enterprise power also encompasses bureaucratic authority based on hierarchical power (reward or legitimate). System-based authority comprises governmental authority, political authority, and academic oligarchy, for example, statewide governing boards. System-based authority tends to operate on reward and legitimate power as well. Last, charisma, which refers to the willingness of a group to follow a person because of her or his unusual personal characteristics, is often associated with a particular president, trustee, or faculty member.

This complicates the issue of power even further. There are not only distinctive power processes used among faculty and administrators, but there are multiple levels of power and authority among trustees, the state, and the occasional charismatic individual. Clark (1991a) even notes another authority that is imposed on the system—the market. Bess gives the following example of the market force: "while faculty may wish to maintain a strong curriculum in, say, aeronautical engineering, if there are too few students willing to major in that subject, the voice of the market will win out over the voice of the faculty" (Bess, 1999, p. 9). However, he also notes that the influences of market forces are themselves ambiguous. Creating change among competing power and authority structures is likely to mean involving a great number of people and political processes, and to happen slowly.

Loosely Coupled Structure

Weick (1991) reminds us that in addition to being interdependent, higher education institutions are loosely coupled. Loose coupling is a cognitive response to an environment of constant change. Within loosely coupled systems, connections, networks, diffusion, imitation, and social comparison are less plentiful or prevalent (Morgan, 1986). Tightly coupled organizations are centralized, nondifferentiated, and highly coordinated, with strict division of labor. Loosely coupled systems are uncoordinated and have greater differentiation among components, high degrees of specialization among workers, and low predictability of future action, including change. Change is flexible, improvisational, and focused on self-design (Weick, 1991). Planned, intentional change as described within teleological models or deterministic and rational evolutionary models are less likely to be successful within this environment.

Weick also notes that major change is less necessary because continuous change is more likely. However, diffusion within the system is disparate; many changes will not be fully integrated across the system. Large-scale change will be difficult to achieve. Due to the level of independence within the system, change is likely to occur in pockets, continuously; independence encourages opportunistic adaptation to local circumstances (Hearn, 1996). Weick (1991) summarizes change in loosely coupled systems as being continuous rather than episodic, small-scale rather than large, improvisational rather than planned, accommodative rather than constrained, and local rather than cosmopolitan; it continuously updates itself. Adaptability refers to changes that meet individual needs, while adaptation refers to changes in response to meeting external needs. Adaptability is characteristic of loose coupling. Although most campuses are loosely coupled, some smaller colleges are able to obtain more synergy between efforts and balance centralized and decentralized activities. Also, community colleges have some centralized controls in place, developing a less loosely coupled system.

During the past two decades, activist trustees, state legislators, and presidents have made attempts to control higher education institutions (Kezar, 2000a). Benchmarking and assessment processes have been put in place. An evaluation of ten years of performance indicators illustrate that they have had modest results. In terms of helping to foster improvement and create change, these indicators have mostly been unsuccessful, inhibiting rather than improving performance (Banta and others, 1996). Efforts to create a less loosely coupled system or to control, centralize, and coordinate have not altered the overall system, which remains loosely coupled. Some state policymakers and national associations are also currently attempting to develop macro-level or transformational changes, but the loosely coupled nature of higher education may hinder these efforts.

Organized Anarchical Decision Making

Within an interdependent system that is loosely coupled and contains multiple power and authority structures, strict lines of decision making are uncommon. Therefore, many commentators have suggested that higher education is an organized anarchy. Organized anarchies have inherently ambiguous goals, unclear technology, and fluid participation, and are uncertain, unpredictable, and nonlinear (Birnbaum, 1991a). Early studies of colleges and universities as bureaucratic systems found that the typical aspects of bureaucratic decision making were missing, such as clear goals, chain of command, hierarchy, and predictable processes. Instead, an organized anarchy is characterized by ambiguity (Clark, 1983a). There is ambiguity about who holds authority in higher education institutions; even though trustees hold the formal authority, over the years, faculty and administrators have developed authority for the organization. Power is ambiguous because, in a collegial system, it is unacceptable to visibly display power. Although some sources of power are clear in the administrative area, this is less true for other parts of the system. Committees, task forces, and other collective groups are involved with much

Power is ambiguous because, in a collegial system, it is unacceptable to visibly display power.

of the institutional policy- and decision making. This anarchical process makes rapid or large-scale change difficult. Understanding change within this type of decision-making process may require social-cognition and cultural models of change that explicate multiple perspectives and shed light on ambiguity. Smaller colleges are less likely than large institutions to have an anarchical decision structure and have been found to be characterized by collegial decision making. In addition, community colleges often exhibit bureaucratic decision-making processes due to the collective bargaining process that more clearly defines faculty involvement in decision making.

As noted earlier, although some activist trustees, state legislatures, and presidents are attempting to gain greater control over institutional policy, there is little evidence that these efforts have resulted in creating any less ambiguity in organizational decision making.

Professional and Administrative Values

A unique characteristic of higher education institutions is that the two main employment groups tend to have differing values systems (Birnbaum, 1991a; Sporn, 1999). Administrative power is based on hierarchy; it values bureaucratic norms and structure, power and influence, rationality, and control and coordination of activities. In contrast, professional authority is based on knowledge and the values system emphasizes collegiality, dialogue, shared power, autonomy, and peer review. Faculty also have divided loyalty between disciplinary societies, professional fields, and other external groups in which they participate (Sporn, 1999). In terms of change, an alteration that appears positive for an individual campus will be viewed through the lens of the faculty member's divided loyalty—for example, in terms of whether the change is important within their disciplinary society or to institutions across the country (Baldridge, Curtis, Ecker, and Riley, 1977).

Professionals are given a high degree of authority and autonomy, with the understanding that they are accountable to each other (Birnbaum, 1991b). In order to ensure this accountability, there is long-term socialization into the profession through graduate school, professional standards, and tenure and promotion processes in which the person has seven years in order to become further embedded in the high standards. Accountability for creating change is part of these standards. Currently, faculty and administrative values are increasingly divergent. Several studies have illustrated more bureaucratization and corporatization among administrative staff (Gumport, 1993; Rhoades, 1995). Administrative staff are coming more often from the business or legal professions than from the ranks of faculty and are suggesting strategies from the corporate sector, such as privatization and outsourcing. Change may be occurring in an environment of growing conflict between administrators and faculty. These values may be illuminated through political and cultural models of change.

> **Change may be occurring in an environment of growing conflict between administrators and faculty.**

Shared Governance System

Higher education institutions are loosely coupled systems, with decentralized decision-making through shared governance processes. Trustees or boards of regents have ultimate governance authority over certain areas of the institution, such as finances, but the major functions and decisions of the institution are shared between the faculty and administrators (Birnbaum, 1991b). Many researchers have described higher education as a collegial institution in which consensus is critical to organizational decision-making and success (Bergquist, 1992). Members interact as equals, minimizing status differences and allowing for greater collective voice and involvement. As noted earlier, power also tends to be informal, through networks of influence. Broad buy-in is necessary; veto power occurs by a small group if they perceive that all voices have not been heard (Baldridge, Curtis, Ecker, and Riley, 1977). In environments where multiple constituents have power, political models of change are usually helpful for understanding and facilitating change. Shared governance is an area that varies by institutional type, as community colleges with collective bargaining systems tend to have less involvement in institutional governance.

Perhaps no other feature has been more demonized in the last decade for slowing down change than shared governance, as a result of the inherently slow pace of consensus-building and collective decision-making (Collins, 1996;

Johnstone, Dye, and Johnson, 1998). Yet this feature characterizes the very nature of the institution and the professional orientation of faculty. Some higher education institutions are trying to move away from their traditional dependence on shared governance, citing the need for rapid change (Johnstone, Dye, and Johnson, 1998). It appears that decisions are occurring more quickly, yet these institutions have not been examined to see if institutionalization of change has been accomplished. Therefore, there is no evidence that change is facilitated by abandoning traditional shared governance processes.

Employee Commitment and Tenure

An obvious but often overlooked feature of higher education organizations is that employee turnover is minimal. Faculty tend to stay in their job for their entire careers because of the tenure system. There are few other organizations with this type of employee stability. In addition, even part-time faculty and contract faculty, noted as a rising percentage of the faculty, also tend to stay at institutions for a long period of time (Finklestein, Seal, and Schuster, 1999). Administrative staff has more turnover, but compared to administrative staff in some other sectors, their tenure is lengthy (Donofrio, 1990). Presidents are likely to have the least time commitment within institutions—approximately seven years (Cohen and March, 1991b). Cohen and March noted the short presidential tenure as one of the reasons that change implemented from the top is less likely to occur, because other employees are willing to stay beyond the plans of any one president or administrator. The long-term commitment of employees and the tenure system have been attacked as reasons that higher education is less likely to change quickly than other institutions. However, institutional commitment is also identified as a critical aspect of organizations that want to create change (within both total quality management and learning organizations). It is unclear whether this characteristic enhances or inhibits the change process.

Several reports predict massive retirement of faculty in the first decade of this millennium. National and state statistics predict that most institutions will turn over approximately 40 percent of their faculty between 2001 and 2010 (Kezar, 2000a). This is a result of the large number of faculty hired as higher education expanded after World War II and during the 1960s in response to the GI Bill and Civil Right's and Women's Movements. This particular decade presents a unique opportunity for creating change on college campuses.

Goal Ambiguity

In describing the anarchical structure, goal ambiguity was noted as a defining characteristic of higher education institutions (Hearn, 1996). Bowen wrote a 300-page book cataloging the major goals of higher education, from critiquing society to enhancing economic development to promoting individual happiness, all complex and multifaceted ([1977] 1997). Bess (1999) identified a shorter set of major goals, but notes their complexity and the difficulty in measuring them. He describes three manifest fundamental social functions: transforming people in terms of cognitive and affective learning, producing knowledge, and public service. Furthermore, different groups embrace various goals in different time periods; thus, learning may currently be the primary goal, but ten years from now production of knowledge may be more important. Cohen and March (1991b) note that there are also inconsistencies between stated goals and actions. Because of the inconsistency between goals and actions, the constantly changing nature of goals, and the need for goals to be placed within specific disciplinary contexts, some argue that these ambiguous goals require professional human resources—highly trained individuals with enough autonomy to respond within this complex environment (Bess, 1999). Change efforts often assume that a clear vision can be established and tied to institutional goals. Yet, since these goals are so unclear themselves, the typical planning process associated with some theories of change might be problematic. Ambiguity of goals could both enhance and inhibit change. Not being clearly tied to a specific or single purpose can make individuals within organizations more open to change.

Currently, some institutions are engaging in efforts to clarify and simplify the goals and outcomes of higher education. This effort is partly the result of state legislators' demands for a better understanding of the primary goals of higher education. However, attempts to clearly quantify goals have been marginally successful (Banta and others, 1996).

Image and Success

There are few bottom-line measures analogous to profit or return on investment for assessing an institution's standing or establishing its competitive advantage (Astin, 1993; Gioia and Thomas, 1996). Under these conditions, the management of image becomes particularly important. Image is generally defined as how members believe others view their organization—and ultimately, how others view individuals within the organization. Image is often tied to identity; to change an image may require a change in identity. The more that people interact and participate in decision-making, the greater their identification with and connection to the organization's image (Gioia and Thomas, 1996). Within a shared governance environment, organizational change may be closely connected with identity modification. Given that identity is central, distinctive, and enduring, change may be a more deeply embedded process, entailing a solid commitment from employees (Cameron and Whetten, 1983). The identity emphasis of change within higher education suggests that life-cycle models (particularly those with a developmental focus) may be an explanatory lens, whereas the emphasis on image and perception might make social-cognition models particularly important to understanding change in higher education.

Some scholars argue that the emphasis on resources and prestige (essentially image) to measure success is problematic; they advocate that student development be used instead (Astin, 1993). Currently, several projects are trying to alter the ways higher education measures success, such as the new Carnegie Classification System and Zemsky's Project on Student Engagement. These projects attempt to move away from image and toward learning outcomes as the measure of success, determining some bottom-line aspects that can be used to define effectiveness. It will be interesting to see if efforts to create clear outcome measures will be successful and supplant the current emphasis on image.

Summary

These unique characteristics of higher education institutions vary by institutional type. The anarchical structure is more prevalent in research universities, shared governance is more prominent in liberal arts institutions, and the power of collective bargaining is key within community colleges (Birnbaum, 1991a). This article tried to illustrate that there is an overall pattern of unique features that characterize the academic enterprise and its institutions, along with their distinctive mission (Hearn, 1996).

In light of these distinctive organizational features, higher education institutions would seem to be best interpreted through cultural, social-cognition, and political models. The need for cultural models seems clear from the embeddedness of members who create and reproduce the history and values, stable nature of employment, strong organizational identification of members, emphasis on values, and the various cultures of the academy. The emphasis on image and identification seem to indicate that social cognition will be important to understand. Furthermore, the loosely coupled nature, anarchical decision-making, and ambiguous goals make meaning unclear and suggest that social-cognition models' emphasis on multiple interpretations may be important to consider when examining change. The shared governance system; organized anarchy; conflicting administrative and professional values; and ambiguous, competing goals also highlight the interpretive power of political models. Evolutionary models will be important for understanding the impact of environmental factors such as accreditation, foundations, and legislatures in an interdependent system, especially since these factors tend to be growing in magnitude and influence. However, even though it is an open system, it may have more internal consistency and logic that can be damaged by the intrusion of external environmental forces. Article five reviews research that has applied the six models within higher education to more comprehensively demonstrate the models' explanatory power.

> **. . . higher education institutions would seem to be best interpreted through cultural, social-cognition, and political models.**

Higher Education Models of Change: Examination Through the Typology of Six Models

IN THIS ARTICLE, research illustrating the application of the six models of change to higher education institutions will be presented. This research review is intended to identify the explanatory power of these models for higher education institutions. There has never been a thorough review of these models summarizing their findings or comparing their abilities to explain the change process. This synthesis will be used to inform and develop the research-based principles on change outlined in article six.

As outlined in article three, there are distinctions among models of change. Some document how it is actually occurring (models evolving from experience), whereas others describe effective approaches or advocate an approach (idealized models). It is important to be aware of this primary distinction in reviewing change theories. Understanding which models best explain the way change is occurring documents current practices. Yet idealized models, even if they have not been effective, may offer solutions to problems or hurdles in the creation of change. The studies presented in this article reflect both types of models—in practice and idealized.

As in the general change literature, teleological and evolutionary models are most prominent within the higher education literature. Political models are much more prevalent in higher education than in the general literature, but life-cycle and cultural models appear to be underused. There is a growing body of research in higher education examining change through a social-cognition perspective. So far, the cumulative evidence suggests that change can best be explained through political, social-cognition, and cultural models. Evolutionary models highlight some key characteristics of change, including homeostasis, interactivity of strategies, and accretion. Life-cycle models have, for the most part, not been applied to higher education institutions, but show promise for helping to develop explanations of how organizational change occurs.

There is mixed evidence about the explanatory power of teleological models, but to date they appear to have limited support from the research in terms of how change actually occurs in higher education and of efficacy for facilitating change. Some strategies have proven successful for creating change, such as incentives or vision. Much of the teleological literature advocates a less political or symbolic approach, describing these approaches as dysfunctional characteristics of higher education institutions. Although political models might explain the way change occurs in higher education, scholars within the teleological tradition argue that political models might not be helpful in facilitating positive change. Teleological theories are often idealized models. The promise within the teleological tradition is that it provides techniques for creating change—which might otherwise not happen—through adaptation, interest-group conflict, or personal development. A general discussion of the application of each category of models is followed by themes that have emerged in the research. Gaps in the research will be elaborated on in article seven.

Evolutionary

Evolutionary models have been applied to higher education institutions with mixed interpretive power. Sporn (1999) provides a comprehensive synthesis of evolutionary models applied to higher education institutions in her book, *Adaptive University Structures*. These models have gained popularity as researchers argue that colleges and universities are vulnerable to the external environment, which is perceived as playing a more direct role in higher education affairs. The proof for these claims lies in recent accountability and assessment movements, performance funding, declining state revenues, public concern that universities are not fulfilling their teaching obligation, and activist trustees (Chait, 1996; Gumport and Pusser, 1999; Sporn, 1999). At this point, there is limited empirical proof as to whether these forces are actually creating change. Instead, there is evidence that resource constraint in the 1970s and late 1980s led to strategies for avoiding change (rather than creating change), such as rapid tuition increases, limitation on student enrollments, ad hoc planning, and budget discipline (Gumport and Pusser, 1999).

The literature on evolutionary models applied to higher education provides useful insights on the following aspects of the change process: (1) change tends to occur through differentiation and accretion (Clark, 1983a; Gumport, 2000); (2) the importance of the concept of loosely coupled systems for understanding change (Clark, 1983a; Rubin, 1979; Sporn, 1999); (3) the need for homeostasis and stability; (4) the limitations of traditional strategic planning (Chaffee, 1983; Keller, 1983; Mintzberg, 1994); (5) the need to negotiate competing forces; (6) the differential impact of environmental conditions on varying institutional types or administrative/academic units (Cameron, 1991; Rhoades and Slaughter, 1997); (7) rapid change is usually the result of resource dependency (St. John, 1991); (8) moderating internal forces to the external environment; and (9) responsive or entrepreneurial universities (Clark, 1998; Peterson, 1995). Overall, these studies appear to illustrate a complex interplay between internal and external forces (Smith, 1993). They demonstrate that the higher education environment differs from other organizations that are highly vulnerable to the external environment, and in which rapid change is common and centralization and high coordination are typical. Instead, homeostasis, internal moderating forces, ongoing change within a loosely coupled system, and resiliency rather than rapid, large-scale transformation are all themes reinforcing a system of midlevel environmental vulnerability (Clark, 1983a, 1993b; Smith, 1993).

Differentiation and accretion: Clark illustrates, in his review of higher education change, that institutions have responded to society and the environment by taking on additional responsibilities and functions, thereby creating new structures (1983a). This process of accretion results in continual addition onto an existing structure that usually remains unchanged, creating greater structural complexity and differentiation (Gumport, 1993). As the structure differentiates, the organization is fragmented; new pieces are not brought into any coherent, whole institution; and coordination is usually lacking. One study, for example, of the University of California system over a twenty-five-year period demonstrated the process of accretion, by which hundreds of programs, activities, and offices have been added (Gumport and Pusser, 1999).

Loose coupling: The relationship of loose coupling and change was also probably best described by Burton Clark (1983a). Through a historical analysis of change in higher education over the last few hundred years and an examination of institutions worldwide, Clark (1976, 1983a) demonstrates that U.S. institutions have undergone tremendous change, all within loosely coupled structures that often appear disorderly, yet in the end create order. He notes how the disorder of the process leads many to not identify changes that occur within U.S. colleges and universities. The loose coupling has allowed for ongoing adaptive change; for example, adding and subtracting fields of knowledge over time.

Homeostasis: Evolutionary studies also illustrate the importance of homeostasis and the ways in which organizations naturally make adjustments to adapt to their environment (Cameron, 1991; Clark, 1983a; Sporn, 1999). Homeostasis was also a theme noted as critical to nonprofit organizations, which tend to represent long-standing social values. External determinism and radical change, advocated in some teleological traditions and even cultural approaches, are not identified as applicable within higher education (El-Khawas, 2000; Kanter, 1998). El-Khawas examined the university's perception of whether an external influence is constraining or enabling, demonstrating that complex, multiple judgements are made about the relevance of external influences. This complex process of negotiating beliefs about external influences tends to emphasize a slow, iterative, constant change, moving toward homeostasis. Clark's work on loose coupling also suggests that continuous adaptation is related to the need for homeostasis at institutions (1983a, 1996b). This suggests that measured and continuous approaches to change are probably favorable within this institutional context.

Strategic planning: Strategic planning focused on external threats and challenges has been found to be mostly unsuccessful in higher education (Birnbaum, 2000; Chaffee, 1983; Keller, 1997). For example, adaptive strategy focusing on scanning market conditions, reporting trends to authority figures, and having an external focus appears to be less successful in higher education (Chaffee, 1983). Interpretive strategy, which focuses on norms and values and the use of orienting metaphors, is more successful. In other words, external circumstances must be translated and compared to internal norms. Rather than reacting to or changing due to the environment, employees tend to process external forces. In addition, many studies on planning conclude that it must be coupled with collegial forms of decision-making, information-sharing, and other cultural or cognitive processes in order to foster to change (Cameron and Tschichart, 1992). One major advancement in recent years has been the strength of planning models that incorporate fluid and unpredictable environments and assume a less rational approach. Strategic planning developed within the evolutionary tradition has been more successful than the deterministic and rational models of planning within the teleological tradition, which will be described on pages 107 and 110.

Competing forces: The external environment has been demonstrated to be a factor in creating change on college campuses. Several studies have examined the impact of capitalism (or market forces) on higher education institutions, particularly in reorganizing the work of faculty and resource allocation in colleges and universities worldwide (Gumport and Pusser, 1999; Rhoades, 1995; Rhoades and Slaughter 1997). Changes noted over the past few decades are the growth of part-time faculty, the development of technology transfer units the growth of certain disciplines that can create resources for the institution and the decline of others, and moving toward a loss of community. Market forces tend to enact slow change, over time, but have been illustrated to impact institutions in profound ways (Rhoades and Slaughter, 1997). Even though change tends to be internally defined, external forces are always slowly altering the shape of the river (Gumport and Sporn, 1999). The river analogy is used to describe the way that external forces interact with these long-standing institutions. Thus, any institutional change process must contend with and reconcile changes that are already being created by the external environment.

> **The external environment has been demonstrated to be a factor in creating change on college campuses.**

Differential impact of environmental factors: Some scholars have illustrated that institutional type determines the type of change approach that will be efficacious. For example, Cameron (1991) suggests that adaptation models are critical for liberal arts colleges, which are more dependent on fluctuations and changes in the external environment—market forces related to tuition and competition, for example. Community colleges and urban institutions have been shown to be more environmentally vulnerable, given the heavy influence of local communities and boards on decision-making and resource allocation. Another example is that changes in the community, such as a depressed economy, hurt these institutions more than other types of institutions (Baldridge, Curtis, Ecker, and Riley, 1977). Evolutionary models will probably have stronger explanatory power within these two sectors in particular.

In other studies, the impact of market forces on different departments is examined in relation to university restructuring (Gumport, 1993). Departments with a greater ability to attract external resources (business or engineering) are more likely to excel than divisions (humanities or education), faculty, and programs that are less attractive to obtaining external resources (Rhoades and Slaughter, 1997). Although few studies have been conducted, they do present some of the greatest promise of this line of research, illustrating that certain sectors or units are much more vulnerable to the external environment. This also helps to predict a future in which public higher education might become influenced by these forces and provide needed data about successful responses to environmental changes (Gumport and Pusser, 1999).

Resource dependency and intentional transformation: Studies of rapid transformational change within higher education tend to document responses to extreme financial conditions, leading to retrenchment, for example (Cameron, 1983a, 1983b; Davies, 1997; St. John, 1991). Few colleges or universities undergo rapid change unless there is a crisis; most often, the crisis is financial. Occasionally, a cultural crisis may result in a rapid response or change such as an extreme act of discrimination (Kezar and Eckel, forthcoming). Recent studies of intentional transformational change in higher education illustrated relatively poor results, with only six of twenty six institutions making progress after five years (Cameron and Quinn, 1988; Kezar and Eckel, forthcoming). Of the six institutions that created transformational change, most made significantly less progress than they had targeted. These institutions faced some formidable external challenges, including legislatures that were critical of higher education, performance indictors, reductions in funding, enrollment declines, and poor accreditation reports, but these did not pose strong enough threats to foster second-order change. Without extreme external circumstance, especially financial challenges, the change process tends to be slow and adaptive (Kezar and Eckel, forthcoming).

Moderating forces to the external environment: Some studies have illustrated that the external environment is less significant on college campuses than within other sectors. Studies using the sensemaking (social-cognition) lens have demonstrated that organizational participants tend to interpret external environments through internal mechanisms. The external environment is clearly influential, but organizational sensemaking creates a context for interpreting the external environment (Gioia and Thomas, 1996). For example, if resources are constrained in the external environment, administrators will interpret this change and its implication through their view of the identity and image of the institution. If they feel it is a top institution, then they feel no threat, even though the real situation of constraint exists. Sporn (1999) found that adaptation may be triggered by external demands, but they are defined internally as a crisis or opportunity by the institution.

One study examined utilitarian (institutional actions and decisions aim at dealing with a competitive environment) versus normative (de-emphasizes external market orientation) identities (Smart, Kuh, and Tierney, 1997). Fewer institutions perceived themselves as utilitarian; many more saw themselves as normative, reinforcing the finding that change appears to be mostly influenced by internal, not external, factors. Smart and St. John (1996) also conducted a study that illustrated essentially the same findings: that institutions are typically normative in orientation. Their findings also suggested that a nonmarket orientation made an institution more effective than a market or external orientation. Market-oriented campuses lost sight of their mission, created unstable environments, and negatively affected personnel. These studies reinforce the earlier evolutionary themes: the external environment can be a catalyst for change, but the internal environment appears to temper this, perhaps working toward homeostasis, which appears healthier for these institutions.

Responsive and entrepreneurial institutions. There is a long line of research that tries to illustrate that colleges and universities are adaptable (or should be adaptable) to the environment (Sporn, 1999). The newest incarnation of these ideas is the notion of the entrepreneurial or responsive university. Clark's recent study (1998) examines institutions that are responsive to the external environment, studying what characteristics allow this interactivity. The model assumes that an externally oriented mission is positive. Some of the principles characterizing an entrepreneurial university are new organizational values and ideas that are strongly interconnected to the structure, academic departments fusing new administrative capabilities, contract education and consultancy, outreach administrative units promoting contract research, and diversifying income (Clark, 1998). Peterson proposes four processes for achieving the status of a responsive university: redefine the university's nature and industry, redirect external relationships and missions, reorganize processes and structure, and reform university culture (Sporn, 1999). Both entrepreneurial and responsive models suggest that being externally oriented is critical to some campuses' mission and provide ways to maximize an external orientation. Even though there has been minimal research on responsive or entrepreneurial universities, they are becoming increasingly prominent in the literature. They are an extension of a long line of idealized models that attempt to provide direction for higher education as it tries to balance internal and external claims in the change process (Keith, 1998).

Teleological

Teleological models have had mixed results in terms of helping to explain change in higher education. Certain concepts have been successful, such as creating a vision or planning. However, many of the specific models, such as TQM or reengineering, have been applied with limited success, especially to changes in the core of the institution—among the teaching and learning processes (Birnbaum, 2000). Birnbaum (2000) and Bess (1999) offer a host of reasons for poor results, including the inability to clearly state the missions and goals of institutions, unique planning problems, lack of centralized decision-making, short-term orientation of teleological models, or the inertia of long-standing structures. Furthermore, ambiguity—noted above as one of the fundamental characteristics of colleges and universities—suggests that planned change models, with their emphasis on rationality, linearity, and clarity of process, are unlikely to be successful within the higher education system. Perhaps not surprisingly, the teleological model that has been applied most in higher education—total quality management—advocates a more collective and consensual process. Within certain units on college campuses that operate under a more businesslike approach, teleological models have been effective (Eckel, Hill, Green, and Mallon, 1999).

There is a tremendous amount of advocacy literature claiming that these models—especially organizational development, rational planning, TQM, reengineering, and restructuring—have been successful for individual institutions (Alfred and Carter, 1996; Balderston, 1995; Benjamin and Carroll, 1996; Dominick, 1990; Elton and Cryer, 1994; Farmer, 1990; Morris, 1994; Nevis, Lancourt, and Vassallo, 1996; Norris and Morrison, 1997; Slowey, 1995). Advocates of teleological models tend to recommend a particular change such as a focus on customers or efficiency. Little of this literature actually studies change processes to identify how it occurs; rather, the authors advocate that change should occur within these models and then study institutions that have chosen to implement these approaches (Levin, 1998a; Meyerson, 1998; Slowey, 1995). More empirical research studies are needed to demonstrate the viability and usability of these models.

The themes that emerge related to teleological models are mission, vision, strategic planning, focus on leadership, incentives, interrelationship among strategies, narrower efficiency and cost emphasis, and limited success of models. The core lessons from teleological models are so ingrained in administrative thinking that we might often forget that these ideas have not always existed to guide change processes; for example, rethinking the mission and tying institutional incentives to mission (Eckel, Hill, and Green, 1998; Lindquist, 1978); establishing a planning process with specific goals (Keller, 1983); strategic planning processes that not only ensure that planning processes are tied to the mission, but also take into account environmental factors (Keller, 1983); and establishing a vision to serve as a guide for change processes (Eckel, Hill, Green, and Mallon, 1999). These concepts are described below.

Mission and objectives: Having discussions related to mission has been found to be effective in facilitating a change process, especially at the beginning (Dominick, 1990; Eckel, Hill, Green, and Mallon, 1999; Lindquist, 1978; Nordvall, 1982). Several teleological change models emphasize the importance of mission, including organizational development and rational planning models. Lindquist's work suggests that the evolution of the change vision should be strongly tied to the mission (1978). The mission also ties naturally (or should) to any strategic planning efforts. Management by objectives (MBO) was a major strategy advocated for creating change that focused on the missions and goals of organizations. By clearly delineating the objectives of the organization and communicating these objectives to employees, the manager could create needed change (Nordvall, 1982). Although an important principle, colleges often find it difficult to develop a mission and set of objectives that are shared by people throughout the campus (Birnbaum, 2000).

Vision: Probably the most commonly described strategy within change is a motivating vision; it is also highly interrelated with other organizational activities such as planning, institutional communication, leadership, reward structures, and hiring processes. Vision has been identified as central to both implementing and accomplishing change (Kaiser and Kaiser, 1994; Kerr, 1984; Mathews, 1990; St. John, 1991). The literature identifies why vision is so critical: change often invites risk and an uncertain future or destination, so having a compelling reason is crucial. A motivating vision can become the blueprint or compass for many employees, allowing them to move toward something new and unknown. Attempts to develop a truly shared vision for an entire institution with such different values, with ambiguity about goals, and a loose structure have proven to be unsuccessful in many cases (Chaffee, 1983).

> **. . . change often invites risk and an uncertain future or destination, so having a compelling reason is crucial.**

Strategic planning: Tied closely to the notion of mission, objectives, and vision is strategic planning, which has also been found to create change on college campuses (Cameron and Quinn, 1988; Daoud, 1996; Kezar, 2000a; Meyerson, 1998; Norris and Morrison, 1997). As noted in the section on evolutionary models, planning models have been proven to be successful in providing some structure to the change process, and are shown to be most successful when coupled with other cultural and/or interactive strategies (Eckel, Hill, Green, and Mallon, 1999; Nordvall, 1982; Peterson, 1997; Taylor and Karr, 1999). Several authors have critiqued traditional strategic planning, debunking it as a linear process, questioning its predictability, and dispelling its efficacy and rational approach (Mintzberg, 1994). For example, one study found no significant differences between the fiscal conditions of institutions before and after planning began, between planners and nonplanners, or between minimal and intensive planners. On average, more positive (though not statistically significant) change in fiscal condition was experienced by the nonplanning institutions (Swenk, 1998). Although some studies have found that strategic planning efforts fall short and do not always create change, some campuses are successful in using planning for change; thus, there are mixed results (Taylor and Karr, 1999).

Focus on leadership: It is widely acknowledged in the literature on change that support from the president and other individuals with positional power promotes the change process because they can secure human and financial resources and focus institutional priorities (Cowan, 1993; Farmer, 1990; Kerr and Gade, 1986; Lindquist, 1978; Lovett, 1993). Although grassroots change can occur, especially on campuses with strong faculty or student groups, these change efforts can be met with resistance if there is not buy-in from those with positional power (Kerr, 1984). Even though colleges and universities have been described as organized anarchies (Cohen and March, 1991a) where change can happen haphazardly without leaders (or often not at all), several studies have illustrated that change was facilitated through the support of individuals in positions of power (Birnbaum, 1991a; Eckel, Hill, Green, and Mallon, 1999; Kerr, 1984).

Within the past ten years, a willing president or strong leadership seems to be waning in importance compared with organizing collaborative leadership (Clark, 1996a; Cowan, 1993; Curry, 1992; Bensimon and Neumann, 1993; Lindquist, 1978; London, 1995). Collaboration typically involves stakeholders throughout the organization in aspects of the change process, tying into the shared governance structure and work of committees. The optimal degree of collaboration necessary for facilitating change is unknown. Sometimes collaboration entails vision-setting; other times, collaboration means allowing people voice, but no real authority over direction, goals, or process. However, some studies have found that campuses become embroiled in discussions around vision-setting and never get to implementation (Birnbaum, 2000). Although not clearly understood, collaboration's impact on change appears to be significant in terms of commitment, empowerment, engagement of individuals with thorough knowledge of the institution, and development of momentum (Gardenswartz and Rowe, 1994; Kotter, 1996).

Incentives: Rewards or incentives have been identified in many different studies as ways to encourage employees to channel efforts from existing activities to new or additional activities (Eckel, Hill, Green, and Mallon, 1999; Mathews, 1990; Roberts, Wergin, and Adam, 1993; Tierney and Rhoades, 1993). The range of incentives may include computer upgrades, summer salaries, merit increases, conference travel money, and public recognition and awards (Eckel, Hill, Green, and Mallon, 1999). Although a motivating vision or mission provides people with a compelling reason to engage the change process, incentives can provide vehicles for continuing or enabling change. For example, employees might want to be part of the change process, but need new skills. Enabling them to attend a conference on assessment might be the necessary incentive to have them be able to facilitate change (McMahon and Caret, 1997). However, many studies also show that faculty are generally not motivated by external rewards, and most change is thus the result of internal motivators (Bess, 1999; Blackburn and Lawrence, 1995). So the extent to which incentives create change among faculty and professional staff is not clearly understood.

Interrelationship among change strategies: Recent studies have illustrated the connection and interrelationship among change strategies (Kezar and Eckel, forthcoming). Much of the early, nonresearch-based literature presents change strategies as isolated actions (rather than linked or bundled) and occurring linearly, not viewed systematically (Cowan, 1993; Kaiser and Kaiser, 1994; Roberts, Wergin, and Adam, 1993; Taylor and Koch, 1996). For example, it is advised to first develop a vision, then to communicate the vision, obtain buy-in, and to develop an implementation plan. Findings within newer studies illustrate that strategies happened simultaneously and in support of eachother (Birnbaum, 2000; Kezar and Eckel, forthcoming). Taking action helps to build collaborative leadership, while senior administrative support enhances collaborative leadership. Realizing that strategies are interconnected and nonlinear increases institutions' success in the change process (Kezar and Eckel, forthcoming).

Narrower efficiency and cost emphasis: Many of the recent teleological change models have had a strong orientation toward efficiency and cost containment. Restructuring, business process reengineering, and outsourcing are examples of three recent change models that focus specifically on ways to restructure operations in order to achieve cost efficiencies (Burton, 1993; Kezar, 2000a). The main techniques used include downsizing the number of employees, streamlining processes, and rethinking the ways that systems operate. It is not surprising that these models emerged in a time of economic challenge and greater international competition. Within these models, change is characterized as a necessary reaction to external threats and to increased competition. Some commentators note that teleological models of change may be dangerous to the overall system, hurting its long-term response, as they move higher education toward an efficiency model that alters goals and professorial autonomy (Bess, 1999; Birnbaum, 2000). Long-standing institutions can damage their roles in and contributions to society by reacting to short-term market conditions.

Limited success in facilitating change: Several different studies have found that TQM has failed based on its inability to incorporate academic values (Birnbaum, 2000; Freed, Klugman, and Fife, 1997). Other studies of strategic choice found that institutions that utilized this approach for planning change of financial resources were worse off than institutions that did not use the model (Kezar, 2000a). Also, in Gioia and Thomas' study (1996), the ambiguity of goals made strategic planning and decisions related to change mostly useless and political sensitivities much more important. The unique characteristics of higher education are in conflict with the assumptions of teleological models, which assume a clear vision, unambiguous plans, a decision-making chain of command, clear delegation of responsibility, decisions based on facts, and rationality (Benjamin and Carroll, 1996; MacTaggart, 1996).

Studies need to examine the application of teleological models to understand why they do not work as well as intended. Perhaps through an analysis of institutions struggling to adopt models that do not succeed, research can develop more applicable teleological change models. For example, studies of strategic planning have found that when coupled with cultural change approaches, such as using metaphors to connect the plan to the history and traditions of the institution, it can be successful (Chaffee, 1983).

Life Cycle

There have been virtually no studies of life cycle or developmental change within higher education, making it difficult to assess the viability of these models. Cameron and Whetten (1983) suggest a model of the relationship between organizational life cycle and institutional adaptation, focusing on how institutions will respond uniquely, depending on their life stage; this model still needs to be tested. Change processes may occur uniquely depending on the organizational life cycle of a college or university. Levine (1998) suggests that higher education institutions are a mature industry; this means that change is likely to occur uniquely, based on the stage of organizational life cycles within which it occurs. As mentioned in article three, in a mature industry, change tends to be slower and less radical, whereas change in a young organization tends to be rapid. Levine does not provide empirical proof, and no one has studied this issue. Research studying different life spans of varying institutional types, such as community colleges versus state colleges or liberal arts colleges, is an important future direction. Institutions that have been around for varied lengths of time might be compared. A few researchers have studied organizational decline, particularly in the late 1970s when some higher education institutions were experiencing severe retrenchment (Cameron and Whetten, 1983; Goodman, 1982; St. John, 1991). These studies help to understand factors causing stress and crisis among institutions and have developed institutional indicators of danger, such as overexpansion during good times, but have done little to further our understanding of the change process.

There has also been limited research about developmental models. One study examined the change process as akin to identity development, paralleling psychological theories of image formation (Gioia and Thomas, 1996). It was postulated that successful organizational change is a reflection of facilitating the individual's change in his or her image. Alteration in identity development or image was found to be closely associated with the language of change, reasons for change, and outcomes of change processes. Higher education institutions have distinctly human-oriented characteristics: community is often centermost, the services provided are teaching and learning, and the client often stays on the campus as part of the community. This human focus makes the importance of identity more apparent. Identity involves a long-term, complex kind of change. Life-cycle models may help us to better understand how to facilitate this type of change because they assume that buy-in, support, and training are probably key to long-term developmental processes. One cautionary note in studies of change is that senior administrators in higher education tend to assume that identities are somewhat fluid, more so than most theories of identity would allow (Gioia and Thomas, 1996). Because identity appears to be so important to the higher education enterprise, these models may provide some useful explanatory power.

A few studies found individual motivations, attitudes, feelings, and behaviors as the key factors facilitating or hindering change (Aune, 1995; Austin, 1997; Farmer, 1990; Nedwek, 1998; Neumann, 1993). Unfortunately, this is an area with few empirical studies—mostly anecdotes from campus leaders—so it is hard to draw conclusions. It also seems significant that almost every anecdotal report notes that institutional change is dependent on individual transformation and growth, often through staff development. The findings of life-cycle theories relate to the concept of learning organizations in which the critical element of change is learning or development among individuals within the organization. Life-cycle and developmental models remain an important area for future research.

Dialectical

Over the past three decades, several dialectical change models have emerged in higher education. These models appear to have strong explanatory power for understanding the way change occurs in higher education. In addition, they help to demonstrate strategies for effectively facilitating change. Some key findings include (1) the importance of interest groups and power within colleges and universities for creating change; (2) persuasion and influence strategies; (3) the significance of informal processes within change, such as behind-the-scenes conversations and deal-making, (4) the efficacy of persistence, (5) the role of mediation; and (6) the manner in which politics prevents change.

Many of the key findings related to dialectical models were found by authors studying other theories. These researchers were struck by the level of coalition-building, interest groups, negotiation, and informal processes. These findings were especially compelling, because people who were trying to illustrate the power of paradigms, culture, the environment, or planning concluded, at times to their dismay, that political processes created change (Gioia and Thomas, 1996; Simsek and Louis, 1994). This should not be surprising given the analysis of higher education organizations offered in article four; as Burton Clark noted, "the many offices, divisions, and schools, protect specialized interests as do the many chairs, departments and faculties in the field" (Clark, 1983a, p. 214).

Some researchers criticize political models' relevance to all institutional types in higher education, suggesting that smaller institutions may have less political environments. Others note that many of the studies that identified political forces were developed in the 1960s and 1970s, a time when the country, and higher education itself, was more politicized (Baldridge, Curtis, Ecker, and Riley, 1977; Gumport and Pusser, 1999). Yet political models have been shown to be just as relevant within today's university (Hearn, 1996; Sporn, 1999). Hearn noted that most studies of change (or of higher education organizations in general) identify staking out positions, forming interest groups, establishing alliances and coalitions, putting the right spin on issues, and manipulating symbols as characteristics of the higher education organizational setting and the change process. Even Simsek and Louis (1994), who studied paradigm shifts and examined change through a cultural approach, found coalition-building on the part of university leaders as one of the most prominent aspects leading to and characterizing change.

Interest groups and power: A specific dialectical model of change was developed for higher education by Clifton Conrad (1978) in a qualitative, grounded theory examination of a number of institutions engaged in change. He found that change occurred based on the interest and goals of powerful groups. The study found conflict existing within all college environments studied; conflict translated into pressure for change. Conflict is heightened by the clash of different interest groups, then is transformed into policy that reflects the powerful interest group. Gioia and Thomas (1996) examined strategic change in academia, also through a grounded theory approach, and determined that political issues were central to the change process. Conflict, interest groups and factions, competing interests, difficulty in discussing resources, and especially differential allocation were noted as catalysts for change.

Burton Clark (1983a) suggested that political processes were at the heart of change in academic institutions. Institutions change as a result of the self-interest of individuals and groups around differentiated specialties and the organizational parts that support and carry them. Clark saw this process as tied to the splintering of knowledge, creating more interest groups and resulting in new academic structures such as additional departments. Yet existing groups defend the resources and power they already have, creating conflict. The following quote illustrates the way interest groups and power have been represented in higher education institutions:

> *We depict the situation as a seesaw, a long board on which reform-supporting and reform-opposing groups sit at different points in relation to the center of balance, far out toward the end or close to the center according to the extremity of their views. If all groups were equal power, the seesaw's direction would depend on how many groups were located on either side of the balance, and particularly the intensity of their commitment. But some groups are genuine heavies in terms of power whereas others are lightweight. . . . When the (heavies) assert themselves, they can throw the weaker innovative groups off the seesaw, leaving them dangling uncomfortably in midair, or force them to declare that the game is over [Clark, 1983a, pp. 225–226].*

More recently, political studies of change examine the growing separation between administrators and faculty; administrators are focused on reorganizing faculty work and roles, creating more tension and deeper divisions among interest groups (Gumport and Pusser, 1999; Rhoades, 1998). Several studies have noted the growing managerialism and collective bargaining and power struggle emerging between the faculty and administrative ranks. Higher education appears to be in a period of growing conflict and interest-group mentality. Power has been illustrated to be a major driving force among interest groups as well as a major catalyst for (or against) change on college campuses (Baldridge and Deal, 1983; Clark, 1983a; Conrad, 1978). As noted in the section on the distinctive characteristics of colleges and universities, power is highly diffused within this environment; this means change occurs at many different levels and is more likely to be decentralized.

> **As a result of diffuse power, persuasion and influence have been found to be important to creating change.**

Persuasion and influence: As a result of diffuse power, persuasion and influence have been found to be important to creating change. In many organizations with centralized authority, power is usually in the hands of those in formal positions of authority. Since colleges do not operate in this manner, persuasion and influence are main tactics for asserting power. Baldridge, Curtis, Ecker, and Riley's (1977); Conrad's (1978); Clark's (1983a); and Gioia and Thomas' (1996) studies found that interest groups are motivated primarily by protecting their resources, structures, and other aspects they see as fundamental to their existence, and that their main tactics for protecting their interests include persuasion and influence. Studies have identified forms of persuasion associated with creating change specific to higher education. These tactics differ from those of other organizations and focus on three main types: manipulation of symbols or meaning, one-on-one informal communication, and appeals to expertise (Conrad, 1978; Childers, 1981; Walker, 1979) An example of manipulation of symbols is for a department chair to invoke the school logo and theme to obtain support for an initiative. One-on-one informal communication will be described in detail later. An appeal to expertise would be to suggest a curricular modification and then to describe how a disciplinary society supports this type of change.

Coalition-building: Many studies of change have found that coalition- or alliance-building is an effective means for bringing together interest groups and creating a power base (Baldridge, Curtis, Ecker, and Riley, 1977). Because of the high degree of ambiguity on campuses and the diffuse power base, strategies for creating change tend to be highly visible and include a large number of people, especially influential individuals. Influential people are defined differently on each campus, but examples include people with seniority, people who have a reputation for fairness, people who bring in large number of resources, and individuals with external prestige. Coalition-building also represents a strategical way to bring people together on a temporary basis, with little extra effort, as no new offices, structures, or resources are needed to develop a coalition or alliance. Coalition-building has been found to be one of the most effective strategies for creating change (Baldridge, Curtis, Ecker, and Riley, 1977).

Informal processes: Influence or power exerted through informal groups, processes, and committees has been illustrated to have a significant impact on change (Baldridge, Curtis, Ecker, and Riley, 1977; Gioia and Thomas, 1996). Informal processes are difficult to study, but each study of change through a political lens have found that informal discussions, one-on-one deal-making, or hallway negotiations are often among the most effective strategies for creating change, especially rapid change (Hearn, 1996). An example of an informal process might help make this finding more understandable. Two administrators, anytime they ran into colleagues, delivered the same message about the importance of peer evaluation of teaching. It was never the main topic of conversation, but was dropped into discussion casually each time. Over the year, the school began to see profound changes from this informal process of persuasion. This area needs further study; the findings are mostly suggestive, or the studies are unable to really judge the effectiveness of this process relative to others in the study of change. Related to the importance of informal processes was the notion of persistence—that is, people who are willing to work behind the scenes for long periods of time.

Persistence: Because higher education institutions are ambiguous and complex environments, they are vulnerable to people who will spend time, be persistent, and advocate for a change, since most short-term efforts tend to get lost in the system (Baldridge, Curtis, Ecker, and Riley, 1977; Cohen and March, 1991a; Hearn, 1996). Hearn notes that "those that are vocal, willing to attend regular committee meetings, willing to take on seemingly mundane tasks, and willing to meet with administrative leaders can achieve far greater effectiveness" (1996, p. 146). All the studies of change through a political framework discovered that individuals, groups, or coalitions that continuously brought up an idea and provided ways to implement it were the most likely to make change occur.

Mediation: Another strategy that is often used to create change among the interest groups, conflict, and power is mediation (Baldridge, Curtis, Ecker, and Riley, 1977; Baldridge and Deal, 1983). Administrative leadership often acts as a mediator, brokering various competing claims (Conrad, 1978). Mediation appears to happen at levels throughout the institution, among individual faculty, departments, schools, and groups within the university. Collective bargaining is an example of a mediation process among faculty and administrators. Several studies have suggested that higher education institutions need better mechanisms of mediation or negotiation, especially because power is so diffuse; there are often limited ways to weigh various claims or rights. Others fear that this will be another factor eroding community on campus. Both Clark (1983a) and Conrad (1978) found that mediation needs to be better understood as a facilitator of change.

Preventing action: Political processes were noted as preventing strategic action and possibly subverting change processes (Gioia and Thomas, 1996). If issues were labeled as political—such as student involvement in governance, diversity, or administrative structural changes—then there was limited or no activity on these items. Gioia and Thomas noted that political issues are important because they point to previously overlooked strategic possibilities and untenable political states that might be left alone. Political processes appear to stifle as well as to create change (Clark, 1983a; Cohen and March, 1991a; Conrad, 1978). However, the finding that certain issues are identified as political and then not acted upon is insightful as to why some changes proceed more quickly than others. It also helps campuses to know what change initiatives might be mired in difficulties and to try to create strategies to address campus discomfort. Many campuses, for example, struggle to institutionalize diversity; the finding that diversity is considered a political issue and that cannot be easily addressed might help develop an awareness that can break the tension.

Many administrators may be quick to resonate with this last finding that political processes deter change and diminish planning efforts or strategy. However, what these findings make clear is that political processes are extremely effective in creating change. In addition, these strategies may be more likely to create change quickly through informal processes (Hearn, 1996).

Social Cognition

Use of social-cognition models, especially models of learning organizations, is growing among scholars within the higher education literature. An appeal of these models is that they accommodate the ambiguous environment of higher education. For example, social-cognition models tend to emphasize discussion and learning among institutional participants, helping them to understand the change process. These models illustrate that campus employees need to understand what the proposed change is, and that the individuals proposing the change need to further appreciate what the change means for the complex organization. This process of discussion, debate, reframing, and sensemaking is seen as inherent within an ambiguous system and allows for creative outputs to occur (Weick, 1995).

Cognitive reorientation is important to the change process in the following ways: single- and double-loop learning, mental models, constructed interaction, learning organizations, metaphors and language, sensemaking, image, and institutional isomorphism and imitation or emulation. There are two distinct approaches within the social-cognition tradition. Sensemaking, organizational learning, and reframing focus on the importance of meaning construction and making the change initiative meaningful at an individual level. The second major approach is institutional isomorphism, focusing on the way norms and image guide the change process through imitation and emulation. In general, studies within the social-cognition tradition have found the internal environment to be more significant to change than the external forces, with the exception of studies of institutional isomorphism (Weick, 1995).

Single-loop and double-loop learning: Several studies within the cognitive perspective suggest that change in higher education institutions occurs through and can be facilitated by learning (Houghton and Jurick, 1995; Weick, 1991, 1995). Social-cognition theorists have studied two different types of learning: single-loop and double-loop learning. In loosely coupled systems such as colleges and universities, single-loop learning occurs on an ongoing basis (Weick, 1991, 1995). Innovation and change are occurring within departments all the time without transforming the overall system or questioning its governing rules. In addition, innovation can and usually does happen swiftly within local environments, not requiring the massive effort of change throughout the system. Faculty respond to local threats and opportunities resulting from changes in the community, their fields, or departments. However, many changes reach a level at which, if they are to be further diffused, double-loop learning must occur (see pages 44–99 for a description of single- and double-loop learning). The inherent ambiguity of the system makes double-loop learning complex. This is where there is a gap in the literature: What are the best strategies for creating double-loop learning in higher education? Some of the literature suggests that we need to explore our mental models to become learning organizations, which will be discussed next (Senge, 1990).

Mental models: Argyris (1982) and Weick (1991) were among the first to examine cognition and change in higher education institutions, focusing on learning. Soon the notion of learning began to expand into the notion of mental models or cognitive frameworks that shape and frame behavior. Mental models are internal images, assumptions, and stories of how the world works; as Senge notes, "they limit us to familiar ways of thinking and acting" (Senge, 1990, p. 174). The notion of mental models emerged from studies of why organizations (and at times people) were unable to change. In periods of change, new cognitive frameworks (or mental models) are introduced, explored, modified, and adopted (Kezar and Eckel, forthcoming; Mellow, 1996). Leaders are asked to examine their own mental models as they initiate and implement change processes. The difficulty for organizations and leaders is to make employees aware of mental models that will affect their ability to change their behavior (Nedwek, 1998). In other words, obtaining ownership of a vision and communicating it will not be enough to create change, because internal mental models need to be surfaced, examined, and altered (Kezar and Eckel, forthcoming; Senge, 1990). Yet implications are tentative, as there has been little empirical research of this concept in higher education.

Constructed interaction: The notion of mental models is tied closely to constructed interaction. Several studies have begun to examine the role of social interaction for understanding change (Austin, 1997; Gioia and Thomas, 1996; Kezar and Eckel, forthcoming; Weick, 1995). One study of change processes among academic administration surveyed 439 higher education institutions and found that key sensemaking strategies included committees, campus dialogues, reading groups, staff development, and "town hall" meetings (Gioia and Thomas, 1996). These strategies provide opportunities for institutional participants to make new meaning—to help members of the institution change how they perceive their roles, skills, and approaches or philosophies. These studies illustrate that a central component of change is providing vehicles for people to alter their mental models, leading to new meanings and activities.

One approach for fostering constructed interaction uses reading groups or professional seminars. The goal of reading groups is to explore a topic in depth and provide campuses with a common language and knowledge base about a particular issue, such as faculty workload, community-service learning, or campus learning communities (Eckel, Kezar, and Lieberman, 2000). Creating a campus reading group is an intentional strategy to manage the breadth of information, master important knowledge, and involve key people (Eckel, Kezar, and Lieberman, 2000; Kezar, 2000b). Reading groups build on highly developed academic strengths, such as inquiry, focused thought, writing, and contemplation, to advance institutional goals. They complement shared governance; highlight specific elements in ambiguous contexts; uncover institutional assumptions, perspectives, priorities, and biases; and allow people to become aware of differing interpretations of events (Kezar, 2000b; Bensimon and Neumann, 1993; Birnbaum, 1991).

Learning organizations: The work of Argyris (1994), Senge (1990), and Weick (1995) related to learning within organizations and mental models has led to the concept of the learning organization. Several higher education writers advocate the development of learning organizations to create change; however, there has been minimal empirical research, mainly because few universities are learning organizations (Brown, 1997; Brunner, 1997; Kliewer, 1999; Lyons, 1999; Rieley, 1997). One study suggested that one of five main strategies to create transformational change is ongoing staff development, which could be an aspect of a learning organization (Kezar and Eckel, forthcoming). There needs to be more research on institutions that directly link individual and organizational performance, as Senge suggests (Kerka, 1995). Also, because this is mostly a philosophical change by individuals, it is difficult to examine empirically. This remains an idealized model for guiding the change process, rather than a way to understand how change is occurring in higher education.

Metaphors and language: Enabling metaphors and language have been a major trend in the literature on change in the past decade (Kelly, 1998). Bolman and Deal's work on reframing organizations (1991) describes the leader's role as helping organizational participants to understand needed changes through the use of stories or metaphors. Leaders are encouraged to frame issues in different ways so that organizational participants begin to understand the direction in which the institution is heading (see page 53 for further discussion of Bolman and Deal's *Reframing Organizations,* 1991). A recent study of change illustrated that institutional metaphors served as maps for institutional actions and that these maps could be reoriented to create change (Simsek, 1997). Metaphors are also often tied to the image of the organization; thus, they become connected to institutional identity, providing fairly lasting perspectives. Dissemination of metaphors occurs through the social matrix all the time, and there is the possibility that dialogue and interaction will alter images throughout the organization. An example of this process is a provost talking about a research initiative that is undergoing a change. She may note how the previous image was a flowering plant, then replace this metaphor with that of a rocket, because she wants to alter peoples' perceptions of the project as being in a more progressive phase.

Sensemaking: Sensemaking is a bit broader than Bolman and Deal's reframing concept (1991), which is dependent on an individual; in contrast, sensemaking occurs through many different processes and individuals, socially constructing reality together. It is the reciprocal process by which people seek information, assign it meaning, and act (Thomas, Clark, and Gioia, 1993). It is the collective process of making meaningful sense out of uncertain and ambiguous organizational situations (March, 1994b; Weick, 1995). Sensemaking allows people to craft, understand, and accept new conceptualizations of the organization (Smirich, 1983), then to act in ways consistent with those new interpretations and perceptions (Gioia, Thomas, Clark, and Chittipeddi, 1996; Weick, 1979).

Eckel and Kezar's forthcoming study of sensemaking among twenty-six institutions engaged in change processes presents six core sensemaking strategies: (1) numerous, continuous, and widespread structured conversations; (2) use of cross-departmental teams; (3) faculty and staff training; (4) outside individuals or consultants providing ideas; (5) documenting concrete sets of ideas; and (6) public speeches. Structured conversations allowed people to construct new identities collaboratively and openly. Cross-departmental teams led to discussions about beliefs, assumptions, and ideas, because people typically work in silos and are not asked about why they hold particular beliefs. Training brought people together in a social way to learn new skills and meanings about the change process. Outsiders challenged institutional beliefs and assumptions, and allowed for the adoption of ideas from outside that were modified to align with internal values. The creation of documents forced people to talk about assumptions and tended to challenge institutional identity. Last, speaking publicly articulated the institution's identity and how it was shifting.

Another study, by Gioia, Thomas, Clark, and Chittipeddi (1996), reinforces Eckel and Kezar's findings. The tradition of establishing task forces and committees, so common in the change process within higher education, is shown to be a sensemaking process. Committees are an attempt by a set of influential individuals to create metaphors, language, and concepts around the change initiative that could be reframed and retranslated to others. These groups were seen as typically advancing through four different stages: (1) interpretation (attempts by the committee to construct an identity for itself and to interpret the change); (2) definition (floundering, realizing that they are a symbolic tool for the central administration, examination of not taking certain actions, defining themselves only as a launching pad); (3) legitimization (determining how they can exert influence and how much they want to exert, change is starting to become their own vision); and (4) institutionalization (constructing influential statement or recommendations, usually attaching ownership to vision, wanting to develop some level of permanency) (Gioia, Thomas, Clark, and Chittipeddi, 1996). This study shows how institutional processes and structures, such as committees, reorient key individuals' perspectives and commitment in an effort to effect a broader change within the organization.

Image: Image emerged as a key motivator within the change process because the products and services of higher education institutions are mostly intangible. Image was particularly strong among individuals involved in change decision processes. It is suggested that providing "a compelling future image that people can associate with and commit to eases the launching and eventual institutionalizing of strategic change" (Gioia and Thomas, 1996, p. 398). In some studies, image replaced the notion of vision because people could gravitate toward a certain image, a human-oriented term, more than toward some abstract vision (Gioia and Thomas, 1996). Image is also used with alumni to achieve needed resources for change; this group must also buy into the new image and identity, adopting it as their own. This is not surprising, given the attention to image within higher education institutions as a result of their lack of bottom-line goals. Reputation, prestige, status, impression, stature, and visibility were critical concept in facilitating change (Gioia and Thomas, 1996).

Institutional isomorphism, imitation, and emulation: Institutional theory suggests that there are templates for organizing institutions that are implicitly understood and translated to new employees; these templates are interpretive schema, underlying values and assumptions, similar to mental models (DiMaggio and Powell, 1983; Greenwood and Hinings, 2000; Meek, 1990; Scott, 1995). Again, like mental models, templates of institutional behavior create resistance to change. Change processes are identified as means for reinstitutionalizing, altering the dominant belief system. Reinstitutionalization occurs by establishing new normative structures, a process that has been hypothesized to vary in length of time based on factors such as the degree of normative embeddedness, degree of loose or tight coupling, permeability of organization, institutional commitment, competitive or reform environment, degree of enabling pattern, and capacity for action (Greenwood and Hinings, 2000). Because higher education institutions are loosely coupled, have normative embeddedness and high institutional commitment, and generally lack environmental vulnerability, change—especially radical change—is less likely.

One concept within institutional theory that has regularly been applied to higher education institutions to explain change is institutional isomorphism (DiMaggio and Powell, 1983; Gates, 1997; Greenwood and Hinings, 2000).

This concept suggests that institutions do not change as a result of a competitive market, external pressures, or efficiency, but rather through the force of homogenization, striving to be like other types of colleges perceived to be elite (Sporn, 1999). Although various forces move organizations toward homogenization, professionalism or normative forces are seen as critical within higher education (Greenwood and Hinings, 2000). Institutional isomorphism occurs as a means to gain legitimacy and increase survival. Institutions tend *not* to be distinctive in their identity development or image, but to emulate an elite group and institutions they perceive as having the appropriate image or reputation (Gioia and Thomas, 1996). Many different studies have documented how institutions imitate a group of institutions that they consider to be prestigious (research universities) or that are most appropriately conducting a process such as cost containment or exemplary teaching (Gioia and Thomas, 1996; Meek, 1990, 1991; Morphew, 1997). New institutionalism focuses more on interpretation, adoption, and rejection by the individual organization of change ideas, whereas old institutionalism focused more on external factors of legitimacy and less on the internal negotiation process (Czarniawska and Sevon, 1996; Greenwood and Hinings, 2000).

Cultural

Research on higher education change demonstrates the efficacy of cultural models for understanding the change process. However, more research is clearly needed in this area, as many questions remain unanswered and its potential for illuminating the change process is only partly fulfilled. In applying cultural models to higher education, several themes emerged that help to understand this process: the role of history and tradition, symbolism as a strategy to create change, institutional culture affecting the change process, deep transformation and paradigm shifts as uncommon, irrationality and ambiguity as characteristic of the process, and lack of interpretive power of the notion of a culture of change.

Institutional history and traditions: Almost all studies of change in higher education have found institutional history and tradition to heavily influence institutional practices and philosophy and to shape or restrict change (Benjamin, 1996; Birnbaum, 1991a, 1991b; Clark, 1983a, 1983b; Cohen and

March, 1991a, 1991b; Gioia and Thomas, 1996). In Cohen and March's (1974) classic text on leadership and decision-making within an organized anarchy, academic traditions and history, in addition to the ambiguous goals and centralized structure, resulted in leaders having little "direct" influence on change. Several studies of change have illustrated how the campus history and traditions have thwarted change efforts (Clark, 1991a; Kelly, 1998; Miller, 1995). In a few studies, strategic campuses have worked within the history or utilized the traditions to facilitate change (Kezar and Eckel, forthcoming). The implication for the change process in higher education is that the institutional history and traditions need to be understood by change agents and incorporated into the planning process. An awareness of history and traditions can also help to set realistic parameters related to change, as repeated failed efforts to change result in cynicism among employees (Birnbaum, 2000).

Symbolism: Cohen and March (1974) were among the first to point out the importance of symbolism within the college and university change process; this strategy was a reaction to the ambiguous environment of an organized anarchy. As Bolman and Deal note, "faced with uncertainty and ambiguity, human beings create symbols to resolve confusion, increase predictability, and provide direction" (1991, p. 244). Leaders could invoke symbolism to create meaning for people within their environments, often drawing on or relating to the history and tradition of the institution (Clark, 1991b; Dill, 1982; Tierney, 1988). In more recent studies, it is also noted that symbolism can be invoked for creating change (Gioia, Thomas, Clark, and Chittipeddi, 1996). Symbolism is strongly related to change in Chaffee's (1983) research on interpretive strategy, Bolman and Deal's (1991) reframing organizations, and Neumann's (1993) cultural change. These authors discovered that symbolic events could be used as levers for creating change in higher education. Similar to the metaphors and language discussed under social-cognition theories, stories are effective vehicles for convincing people to change their behavior. Symbolic events and activities—for example a kick-off day for a change initiative or campus day of dialogue—enable change initiatives to proceed (Gioia, Thomas, Clark, and Chittipeddi, 1996; Neumann, 1993).

There is some indication that college and university leaders use task forces, committees, events, and ceremonies to disguise what would otherwise be overt power or influence strategies (Gioia, Thomas, Clark, and Chittipeddi, 1996). For example, a president cannot create a change that he decides is necessary for the institution; instead, he has a ceremonial event to kick off a committee and then establishes a group to examine the issue, focusing on philosophy and values. Therefore, there may be some interaction between political and cultural strategies.

Institutional culture: Research illustrates that institutional culture operates at several different levels, shaping the change process (Chermak, 1990; Dill, 1982). Bergquist's study of the four cultures of the academy (1992) shows the relationship between institutional culture—collegial, developmental, negotiating, or bureaucratic culture—and change processes. For example, at an institution where the developmental culture is prominent, training and development are likely to be the main strategies for change, whereas in the bureaucratic culture, planning and assessment would be important. The institutional culture ties not only to the process of change, but to reasons for change. In the bureaucratic culture, change is a response to threats in the environment, whereas on the developmental campus, the need to advance people's understanding would motivate change.

Birnbaum (1991a) and Levin (1998) examined how different institutional types, such as community colleges or liberal arts institutions, have distinctive change processes. The varying institutional types maintain particular cultures and structures; for example, collective bargaining at community colleges can influence the rate of change (Levin, 1998). Kezar and Eckel (forthcoming) demonstrated how unique institutional cultures also shape change processes. For example, an institution that has a history of customer service will reflect responsiveness to students in the strategies, reasons for, and outcomes of change. In a study of the impact of institutional culture on decision approaches, Smart, Kuh, and Tierney (1997) determine that leaders' main mistake is working counter to rather than within the culture in order to create change. Collectively, these studies suggest that institutional type and culture affect the change process and that, in most cases, working within the existing culture facilitates change (Chermak, 1990).

Deep transformation and paradigm shifts: A main area of exploration among cultural models is the notion of deep change that alters the culture of the institution. This deep change is often labeled *paradigm shift* (Simsek and Louis, 1994). Studies of transformational change in higher education illustrate that paradigm shifts are not typical and are extremely difficult to facilitate (Clark, 1983a, 1983b; Kezar and Eckel, forthcoming; Sporn, 1999). Results from the ACE Kellogg study of twenty-six institutions undertaking institutional transformation indicate that few are actually accomplishing the goal of transformational change even after five to ten years (Eckel, Hill, and Green, 1998; Kezar and Eckel, forthcoming). Simsek and Louis (1994) examine cultural paradigm shifts in higher education, finding that paradigm shifts do occur and that change can happen rapidly in higher education as institutions face anomalies or problems in their thinking (similar to Argyris's double-loop learning). But they noted that it appears that higher education institutions tend to incorporate and blend the old paradigm with the new paradigm. Thus, radical change is not really observable. This important finding may point to a direction for future research in which the changes that occur in higher education become more visible; as Clark notes (1983a), most outside observers do not perceive the amount of innovation that occurs within the academy. How do the new paradigm and old paradigm become integrated? The implication for higher education institutions is that they may need to focus more on the integration of old and new perspectives and processes than simply on change initiative.

Irrationality and ambiguity: Cohen and March (1974) and Clark (1976, 1983b) were among the first to illustrate that change in higher education is often thwarted or slowed by the ambiguous environment and, at times, the irrationality. Although ambiguity in goals was discussed at length in article four, the findings about the irrationality of the environment need further explanation. Research suggests that the individual's choice to change is *not* often made based on a review of fact-based data; instead, people are found to consider the implication of the change on the future of their division (political motivations), or based on intuition, or how this change relates to emotional commitments they have made, such as impact on their friends within the organization (Carr, 1996; Clark, 1976). Emotive motivations have been found to be a major factor in decisions to change (Benjamin, 1996; Bergquist, 1992; Neumann, 1993). Intuition, politics, and emotive decisions are typically labeled irrational approaches to decision making.

Culture of change: Although there is little evidence that there is a "culture of change," this remains one of the most popular notions in the literature in higher education (Brown, 1997; Chermak, 1990; Frost and Gillespie, 1998; Parilla, 1993). People advocate for a culture of meaningful communication, clarity of institutional purpose, trust, respect, strong leadership, and teamwork. It is suggested that an environment in which employees feel a sense of self-worth and there is a tolerance for different perspectives will lead to change (Taylor and Koch, 1996). These proposals for a culture of change are usually drawn from Schein's (1985) and Senge's (1990) work. Yet there is limited empirical proof that there is any culture that is more or less encouraging of change. It has also been noted that change is not always good, so it is unclear whether such a culture is functional or allows only positive change to occur.

There is research to suggest that a culture of risk facilitates innovation and adaptability. Many organizational theorists have found themselves deeply embedded in the study of constancy when an understanding of change became elusive. Most literature on constancy reveals that people are unaware of their values or beliefs, which is what makes change so difficult (Argyris, 1982). Constancy is a result of embedded patterns that have become subconscious (Schein, 1985). Staw (1976), for example, studied commitment within organizations. He notes the positive effects of persisting in a line of action that reaffirms previous decisions. To make a different choice questions the wisdom and competence of previous actions and decisions. The result of these findings has been the development of cultures of risk that allow people to change their future actions and approach situations differently (Argyris, 1982).

Multiple Models

Multiple models may respond to some of the unique characteristics of higher education institutions. For example, the dual orientations—professional and administrative—may need different models of change. As noted earlier, multiple models are attempts to draw together the insights and principles from more than one approach.

... multiple models are attempts to draw together the insights and principles from more than one approach.

Robert Birnbaum (1991a) has developed one of the best-known combined models of change in higher education in his cybernetic approach, which includes elements from evolutionary and social-cognition models. The cybernetic model is a loosely coupled, open system in which multiple organizational realities such as the collegium, bureaucratic organization, organized anarchy, and political system exist simultaneously to greater and lesser degrees, depending on the institution. Leaders are encouraged to reframe the way they assess situations and make decisions, integrating the various perspectives through cybernetic controls, which are "self-correcting mechanisms that monitor organizational functions and provide attention cues or negative feedback to participants when things are not going well" (Birnbaum, 1991a, p. 179). As suggested within social-cognition models, leaders are encouraged to look at the institution through multiple rather than one or two frames, because administrators looking at a problem through only one frame have narrow understandings of the problem or proposed change. In addition, as is characteristic of evolutionary models, leaders should avoid action and instead focus on cues within the system (feedback loops), assuring that appropriate monitoring systems are in place, making minor adjustments, and on rare occasions providing intervention on problems. The key role is assessment to determine when change is necessary, allowing the system to take care of itself. The organizational thermostats and feedback loops are features of evolutionary models and reflect ways that living systems provide response (Morgan, 1986), so the change agent's role is to examine the system and not always to respond quickly. Thus, change tends to happen naturally within the system, and when leaders need to become involved they mostly play the role of examining the situation through different cognitive frameworks in order to diagnose the issue and develop a change strategy. Although Birnbaum mentions the political system and culture, these are not major elements of the model or factors that influence change. The efficacy of this model is mostly untested, but it is based on an accumulation of research that supports certain elements of the model.

A model proposed by Lueddeke (1999) within the constructivist tradition attempts to weave the cultural, social-cognition, evolutionary, and teleological models into what is called the adaptive-generative development model (AGD-M). AGD-M was specifically designed to address the unique environment of higher education, in which shared governance is a hallmark and academic values are stressed. The model has six interrelated elements: (1) needs analysis; (2) research and development; (3) strategy formation and development; (4) resource support; (5) implementation and dissemination; and (6) evaluation. The research-and-development component includes a market and external-condition analysis characterizing the university as an open system that needs to monitor its environment, reflecting evolutionary assumptions. Change results from the shared construction of meaning facilitated by a truly inclusive and interactive team, which is the focus of the third step: strategy formation and development. In the stage of strategy formation and development, dialogue and open, critical reflection on the initiative are emphasized. This dialogue is supposed to lead to cultural change. Underpinning the entire model is the notion of learning and the idea that organizations need to go through periods of adaptive and generative learning, characteristics of social-cognition models. The sequential and rational orientation of the model also fits within the teleological model. Many of the approaches, such as needs analysis, research, strategy, resource support, and evaluation, are teleological strategies. Institutions both adapt to external and internal forces and generate solutions to problems; hence the importance of focusing on both adaptive and generative forces.

Summary

When examining how higher education institutions reflect the models of change that have emerged within the multidisciplinary field of organizational change, some valuable research-based principles emerge, which will be summarized in the next article. Some concerns also emerge.

In terms of concerns, people seem to become frustrated by the efficacy of political models for explaining change in higher education. Bureaucratic structures create standards of procedure and policies that can lead to fairness, in addition to providing efficiency and control. There are many protections for individuals within these bureaucratic devices. To acknowledge the highly political nature of change can make higher education participants cynical or suspicious. Yet, as Hearn (1996) notes, to not be aware of the political aspects, even if one rejects that approach, is naïve. For women and minority leaders, in particular, political processes may have been used against them to limit their influence and advancement. To suggest embracing these approaches may seem problematic.

There have also been criticisms over the years about the organized anarchy model and garbage-can decision-making (Kerr and Gade, 1986). If efforts to plan change, especially at the institutional level, are doomed by the ambiguity and complexity inherent in these organizations, then what possible advice can be drawn from these studies? Still, many fruitful models have developed to respond to the ambiguous environment of higher education. Senge's (1990) learning organizations are meant as a response to the multilayeredness and complexity of organizations that were not encompassed in earlier models. I will acknowledge the frustration that can be associated with examining change through some of these models. Teleological models, which appear to empower individuals to create change, tend to be more attractive and feel more comfortable, yet may not be as successful as other models.

Also, there may be frustration related to evolutionary models. They describe forces, such as capitalism or the market, but offer little advice about how to address these deterministic forces (Collins, 1998). Professionals may try to understand how to use cultural or social-cognition models, but find little concrete information to work from. In addition, these models tend to describe the nature of change and do not necessarily address how to facilitate or create change. Often, people find themselves drawn to teleological models, mostly because they can best understand how to apply them to practice.

As noted earlier, choosing a model of change is an ethical and ideological choice; some people may feel more comfortable with certain models than with others (Morgan, 1986). Awareness of the assumptions of models makes it possible to compare them to the reader's own values and develop alignment with an appropriate model. This article does not advocate the value of any one approach, but describes what each model can tell us about the change process in higher education. The next article offers advice about how to draw on each category of models and develop a clearer understanding of change.

Research-Based Principles
of Change

O NE STATIC MANAGEMENT MODEL cannot provide all that is needed to manage the numerous changes that are currently underway in the external environment" (Thor, Scarafiotti, and Helminshi, 1998, p. 65).

The dynamics of change in higher education institutions are complex, and generalizations about change processes are risky. "In fact, the first and foremost fundamental proposition we can stress about change in these settings is so simple as to seem banal and deflating: It all depends" (Hearn, 1996, p. 145).

Hearn (1996) argues in his article entitled *Transforming U.S. Higher Education* that several propositions can be made about change: (1) a political model is important, and even if the participant does not want to use this model, it is naïve not to be aware of the politics that are so prevalent within these institutions; (2) a cultural model is key, and effective change efforts must be integrated successfully into the existing institutional culture and climate; (3) organizations are resource-dependent, and efforts that are not in accord with critical sources of funding, prestige, and personnel are unlikely to succeed; and last, (4) disruption and accretion are both needed. He is one of the few authors who has tried to summarize and apply research about change in higher education and present it to leaders for use on campus. I will attempt the same in this article, having reviewed a larger literature base. The research-based principles described herein are based on the cumulative knowledge of more than thirty years' research. These principles are drawn directly from the meta-analysis conducted in article five, in which theories or models of change have been applied to higher education. In this article, I offer an interpretation of their power to help understand and facilitate change in higher education. Obviously, there are principles that may have not emerged because studies have not yet been conducted; this is certainly the case among life-cycle models of change. That is why article seven, Future Research, is important—it details gaps in the knowledge needed to help deepen our understanding about change processes. However, much can be learned from the cumulative research of the last thirty years. I do not synthesize these principles into a multiple model in order to bring a sense of artificial coherence to the somewhat disparate propositions. Instead, they are offered as issues to consider as the reader engages in change. The problem with any model is the temptation to apply it within all situations; it is not feasible to create a change model for every situation within higher education. Also, I do not divide the principles into the six categories used to organize the previous articles, because most principles are reinforced by studies within several different theories. What made these principles so powerful is that they emerged as significant within many different approaches to studying change. The following are some principles that can be used to think about change systematically and systemically on the reader's campus.

> **The problem with any model is the temptation to apply it within all situations; it is not feasible to create a change model for every situation within higher education.**

Promote Organizational Self-Discovery

The literature surveyed in article four outlines the existing structures of colleges and universities, such as a loosely coupled system, shared governance, and employee commitment. Many studies of change have demonstrated that these structures profoundly affect the change process, especially those within institutional theory. Many change theorists focus on the environment or on individuals as the key factor influencing change. The research in higher education, particularly social-cognition models of institutional theory, demonstrates that the existing structure or internal environment plays a very significant role. If institutions and leaders want to be successful in facilitating change, they need to understand the enterprise and the distinctive nature of higher education that creates this current structure or template. As Burton Clark (1983a) notes, the structure and culture capture the history, habits, and norms that shape institutional practice and philosophies. Simply changing individuals' mental models will most likely not be enough to implement most changes.

Wheatley notes that "the system needs to learn more about itself from itself" in order to allow change to occur (1999, p. 145). She notes that outside experts and small teams are not best for developing this self-understanding— it is best if the whole system is involved. Dialogues, campus summits, reading groups, and other mechanisms that draw people together to talk, relate, and understand issues facilitate self-discovery.

Realize That the Culture of the Institution (and Institutional Type) Affects Change

The research on cultural theories helps us to understand that institutional culture shapes the reason change emerges, the way the process occurs, and the change outcomes. Although many administrators are aware that the institutional culture and type shape organizational life, this may not translate into identifying unique change strategies based on the institution's history, traditions, and norms. It is advisable for institutions engaging in change to conduct an institutional self-audit or assessment of their culture. Although it can be extremely difficult for an institution to comprehend its own culture, there are tools that help to conduct this process, such as consultants or bringing in individuals from other institutions to help provide an outside perspective. However, as Wheatley, notes it is best if the organization comes to this understanding through self-discovery (see Kezar and Eckel, forthcoming). Institutions need to ask themselves questions such as: To what degree are we a collegial, organized anarchy, political, developmental, or managerial culture? The works of Bergquist (1992) and Kezar and Eckel (forthcoming) should help institutions better understand this relationship.

Be Aware of Politics

Savvy change agents should develop an understanding of alliances and coalitions on their campus, who are the heavyweights and people of influence, how informal processes can be used, what conflict exists, what the motivations are behind a proposed change or beyond resistance. In addition, in order to assure that political processes do not hurt particular people or stagnate certain initiatives, it is important to be aware of the way these dynamics are operating. Empowerment approaches can be used to try to ensure that changes treat people equitably. Also, as Gioia and Thomas' study (1996) discovered, certain change issues are more political than others. Their work can help guide campuses in knowing when they áre engaging a particularly political issue. Some readers may be disappointed by the proposition that change is political. It can be argued the current structures and culture reinforce a political model, which can be altered. Some people believe that models such as TQM can work to eliminate a political environment. They argue that the structures and cultures are not themselves political. Dialectical theories suggest that conflict can be overcome, but that this is an extremely rare circumstance. For example, Paulo Friere (1999) described the breaking down of dualistic systems that create political struggles and interest groups. But this idealized vision will, most likely, never come to pass, as it would require hierarchy and power differences to be eliminated; it does not represent the world of current organizations, and certainly not that of higher education institutions.

Lay Groundwork

Almost every theory suggests that self-assessment (social cognition), institutional audits and analysis of the change proposal for institutional compatibility (teleological), awareness of institutional culture (cultural), and reading groups (social cognition) are necessary to become knowledgeable about the change initiative. Most planning processes begin with some form of self-assessment. This groundwork and self-assessment needs to include more people, becoming a collaborative process. It also entails asking the *what* (first order or second order), *how* (revolutionary or evolutionary), and *why* (for student learning or accountability) questions posed in article two. This article can be used to frame such discussions. Also, these discussions might help to defuse poor ideas for change, rather than wasting people's valuable time.

Groundwork should not be laid only for planned or larger-scale change; an environment can be created through groundwork for innovation and promoting generative learning. This groundwork entails ongoing local assessments and conversations.

Focus on Adaptability

Transformational change is unlikely at most institutions, whereas incremental adjustment is pervasive and identified as healthiest for institutions; there was evidence to support this principle across almost every model reviewed (Clark, 1983a). Research from cultural, social-cognition, and political models demonstrated the difficulty of creating deep, pervasive change across the entire institution. Tasks, power, and authority are extensively divided, preventing global change. Second-order or comprehensive change takes a tremendous amount of time and resources, and the chances of it occurring are slight. In general, it is wiser for institutions to invest in innovation throughout the campus and to let great ideas bubble up. If the campus feels it needs to examine curricular incoherence, then supporting a few programs that might want to engage in this type of change is probably a better use of time and resources than trying to initiate comprehensive change, as advocated in much of the recent higher education literature (Eckel, Hill, and Green, 1998). Bergquist (1992) notes that one strategy for planning change is to initiate a first-order, incremental change through temporary education systems (TES) and that if a situation can be established so that the change is aligned with the organization, it can become a second-order change. Experimentation is allowed to occur, ideally within a loosely coupled system.

Change leaders can develop connections among different initiatives and individuals in order to create synergy and provide momentum (Eckel, Green, Hill, and Mallon, 1999). Loosely coupled systems are usually unlikely to have communication, because they are uncoordinated. Informal communication might spread change on the borders, but it is unlikely. Leaders can help to spread the word about good ideas and increase momentum for people on the borders.

Facilitate Interaction to Develop New Mental Models and Sensemaking

The teleological, political, life-cycle, social-cognition, and cultural models emphasize the importance of bringing people together, whether in strategic planning (teleological), committee work (political), staff development (life cycle), or events (cultural), to help employees understand the change, develop new mental models, integrate these models with their existing understanding, and develop a language for articulating the change. In an environment where expert power is predominant, explanation and rationale are important to change. Constructed interaction is the opportunity for creating situations in which the rationales are shared and the new initiative is made open to challenges.

Strive to Create Homeostasis and Balance External Forces with the Internal Environment

Because loosely coupled systems are likely to respond in gradual, perhaps unnoticed, ways to the external environment, direct response should be avoided, at least from some sort of centralized leadership. Leaders should be protectors of homeostasis and intervene only when there is clear indication of a significant problem. And, as the social-cognition and cultural models suggest, the role of leaders should be to facilitate dialogue so that a cognitively complex decision can be made about how to respond to external conditions. An example of this principle is Berdhal's (1991) suggestion that faculty need a stronger voice in helping to prioritize the many requests for campus change. In order to work within and strengthen shared governance, he recommended that a committee should be established to monitor the institution's external relations and to recommend continuity or change.

Some evolutionary studies point to the vulnerability of private colleges, community colleges, and certain departments (for example, humanities). These institutions and departments must be more attuned to external forces. Yet these findings must be tempered with the recognition that, for the most part, the external environment plays a much smaller role in the change process than the internal environment, forces of institutionalism, interest groups, and perceptions about change (Clark, 1983a).

Combine Traditional Teleological Tools, Such As Establishing a Vision, Planning, or Strategy, With Social-Cognition, Symbolic, and Political Strategies

Many studies established that teleological tools were successful for facilitating change when combined with assumptions from other models, using these tools with an awareness of the context, politics, and concerns of individual worldviews and perspectives. Use metaphors, stories, and symbolism combined with planning, assessment, and environmental scanning in order to make the change initiative understandable to people.

Realize That Change Is a Disorderly Process

Change processes that are disorderly often lead to order, and orderly change processes often lead to disorder (Clark, 1983a). The disorderly and at times irrational process that characterizes cultural, social-cognition, and dialectical models not only better explains change, but may lead to more positive change outcomes. Forced orderly approaches such as planning, business process reengineering, or traditional strategy have often failed to facilitate change in higher education (Birnbaum, 2000). However, studies of long-term campus dialogues with no clear strategy have led to fundamental campus changes. Being open to ambiguity and a nonlinear process is important for institutional leaders and change agents.

Promote Shared Governance or Collective Decision Making

Almost every model emphasized the need for working together, particularly, the cultural, teleological, and social-cognition models. Sensemaking, interpretive strategy, and coalition-building are collaborative processes. This principle also aligns with higher education's tradition of shared governance.

Many critiques of higher education have suggested that shared governance is preventing change. In recent years, the response within many institutions has been to create structures that subvert shared governance or to simply allow faculty senates to dwindle. But the research presented herein suggests that a healthy, loosely coupled system that can create change and foster adaptability needs a functional shared governance process and implementation through the joint activities of administrators and faculty (Clark, 1983a; Sporn, 1999).

Articulate and Maintain Core Characteristics

What is it that institutions want to preserve, and why? Almost every model highlighted continuity as important, including evolutionary (homeostasis), social-cognition (institutionalism), teleological (mission-driven) and cultural (importance of traditions and history) approaches. Institutions need to be better able to communicate the importance of core values such as academic freedom or processes such as shared governance to student learning, knowledge production, and service to society and our political systems.

Be Aware of Image

Institutional theory and cultural models suggest that change in higher education has in large measure occurred as a result of institutional image. Clark (1983a) and others have illustrated how many higher education institutions have changed during the last fifty years, mostly becoming similar to America's top research universities because of the prestige these few institutions enjoy— a process known as academic drift. Certainly, this finding has a shadow side; yet it can also be used to create change. Recent movements such as community-service learning have perhaps spread as a result of imitation, following the lead of national organizations such as the American Association of Higher Education and Campus Compact. Therefore, appealing to institutional image and emulation can also be used as a lever for positive change. Institutional legitimacy is a critical force within a values-driven organization such as higher education. Student learning may replace resources for understanding image, but image will continue to be central.

Connect the Change Process to Individual and Institutional Identity

Almost every theory suggests the importance of identity to the change process, especially within institutions like higher education, with strong employee commitment and longevity. In particular, social-cognition and cultural theories emphasize the deeply entrenched beliefs, habits, and norms that coalesce to form identity. Life-cycle theories show promise for providing needed information about identity development and institutional change that might help us in facilitating this process. Teleological models' emphasis on the necessity of discussions related to mission at the beginning of a change process relates to the importance of institutional identity. Change processes in higher education need to engage both institutional and individual identities.

Change processes in higher education need to engage both institutional and individual identities.

Create a Culture of Risk and Help People to Change Belief Systems

In order to achieve stability and efficiency in organizations, we socialize, train, and acculturate people. No wonder that the literature refers to resocializing, re-creating norms, retraining, altering mental models, and reframing cultures. But to ensure change, a culture of risk needs to be developed in which people can feel comfortable making different choices than they made in the past and failure is not penalized. Choosing to act differently questions past behavior, which is mentally trying. Social-cognition models reinforce the need for creating an environment of risk that allows change without blame or reprimand.

Realize That Various Levels or Aspects of the Organization Will Need Different Change Models

No one model may ever encompass the many complex principles related to change, but each serves as a valuable tool for analyzing the institution at different points in time. Bolman and Deal (1991) might help to understand a departmental change initiative, but consulting Birnbaum's (1991a) cybernetic model for a campuswide change might be important for its a strong systems perspective. This monograph can help the reader choose which model to use under varying circumstances.

Another way that models can be used is in combination, for examining different administrative units. Teleological models might work within administrative areas, whereas a political model might best be used within academic affairs. Some units will be more political, while others might be more symbolic. Also, the literature suggests that change can be examined at the broadest level through evolutionary models; the life stage of the organization through life-cycle theories; the intricacies of the organization through cultural approaches; power and interest groups through the political models; and the individual worldviews through social-cognition theories.

Know That Strategies for Change Vary by Change Initiative

Large-scale or second-order change seems to be more aligned with strategies from social-cognition and cultural (and perhaps life-cycle) models, whereas first-order or smaller-scale change appears to be more aligned with evolutionary and teleological models. Changes that are of a values orientation are better approached through a political, cultural, or social-cognition model, whereas structural changes might be better addressed through a teleological or biological model. As noted in article two, institutions need to evaluate the type of change initiative and examine it in relation to the models. In the research, alignment between type of change and approach to change is documented as facilitating change processes.

Consider Combining Models or Approaches, As Is Demonstrated Within the Multiple Models

The multiple models reviewed throughout this monograph illustrate some of the ways in which the principles from various models can be combined to develop a comprehensive and complex approach to change. Birnbaum's (1991a) cybernetic model, Bolman and Deal's (1991) *Reframing Organizations,* and Lueddeke's AGD-M model (1991) can be used as starting places for institutions trying to engage in a change process and examining change through complex approaches. Using the principles as guides, each institution can develop its own combined model based on the type of change, scale of change, institutional structure, environment, and culture. Build a model to suit your campus.

Summary

This article provided guidelines that can be used to develop a model for change based on the particular context of the reader's campus. Here is how the various principles might best be synthesized:

1. Develop a process of systematic, systemic institutional and environmental assessment (guidelines 1, 2, 4, 6, 7, 8, 10, 15).
2. Work with individuals, be inclusive, and realize that this is a human process (guidelines 2, 3, 5, 9, 10, 12, 13, 14).
3. Be aware of the distinctive characteristics of higher education (guidelines 1, 2, 3, 5, 7, 8, 9, 10, 11, 12).
4. Realize the need to develop your own context-based model of change (guidelines 1, 2, 3, 4, 7, 8, 11, 15, 16, 17).
5. Be open to surprises, focus on creativity, and leverage change through chance occurrences (guidelines 3, 5, 6, 9, 14).
6. Balance is an important principle (guidelines 7, 10, 11, 13).

Future Research on Organizational Change

I T IS RARE to find an institution which is at once so uniform and so diverse; it is recognizable in all the guises which it takes, but no place is it identical with what is in any other. This unity and diversity constitute the final proof of the extent to which the university was the spontaneous product of mediaeval life; for it is only living things which can in this way, while fully retaining their identity, bend and adapt themselves to a whole variety of circumstances and environments" (Emile Durkhiem, *The Evolution of Educational Thought*).

How can we better understand organizational change among institutions that have captured the imagination of scholars for centuries? Many aspects of the change process remain elusive. The following section summarizes the main research areas that could help leaders, policy-makers, and institutions to allow higher education to thrive over the next century.

Perhaps one of the most central issues is to determine some of the gaps in our knowledge of change that have been hidden because change has mostly been studied at the overall institutional level, through leaders or in relation to leaders' needs, often without acknowledging the loosely coupled aspects of the system. As Burton Clark notes, change "is widely overlooked since (adaptation or accretion) is not announced in master plans or ministerial bulletins and is not introduced on a global scale" (1983a, p. 113). To what degree is change hidden within a loosely coupled system? Do we really know the amount or level of change occurring within institutions? Much of the existing literature characterizes institutions as unchanging. Could this represent a focus on overall institutional change that is less prevalent within higher education? How can we better capture emergent change processes in departments, divisions, and programs?

There has been a major focus on adaptation in higher education, especially in recent years, as it has been perceived that the academy faces more environmental vulnerability. Yet the literature from organizational theory and on change in higher education institutions suggests that they are much more internally flexible and able to respond than evolutionary models suggest. Perhaps we need to be studying what Weick termed adaptability in higher education. Perhaps our focus on adaptation is headed down the wrong path. What kind of an entrepreneurial organization might emerge if we examined the characteristics of adaptability rather than adaptation, following Clark's recent work? This seems the appropriate avenue for loosely coupled systems with strong internal logic and long histories. Adaptation models' focus on environmental challenges may be important to institutions in crisis, but may not be applicable to the majority of institutions.

Evolutionary research has identified some of the significant forces that can shape higher education, such as resources, the market, and government intervention. However, these models have been unable to tell us why some forces do not have an impact even though they are predicted to influence higher education. For example, why do societal forces (such as calls for diversifying higher education) have a lesser impact than economic forces related to technology? One emerging area in the research is that some institutions will need to focus on the external environment more than others. Is this changing, and are more institutions now vulnerable to outside forces? Few studies have examined accreditors', associations', or foundations' role in the change process. Can campus leaders help encourage change throughout the organization by connecting people to foundations and national organizations that support change around certain initiatives? Usually, the external environment is conceptualized only as a threat; it may be important to study how external forces support change. It is also important to examine the costs of the accretion model of change. Is it vastly more expensive to add on to existing structures, than it is to transform the existing organization. As an analogy, cost-benefit analyses of technology illustrate that bolting on new technology is much more expensive than rethinking the whole system.

Some scholars are suggesting that accretion models may have represented change in the past, but political models might better characterize a time of dwindling resources or Darwinian biological models in times of accountability (Gumport, 2000). Peterson suggests that the past fifty years have been characterized by different types of change that appear to reflect the needs of different eras. The 1950s and 1960s were periods of growth—absorbing new students and expanding institutional boundaries—whereas the 1970s was a time of downsizing, as institutions experienced less growth and students chose different types of institutions for study. The 1980s resulted in reorganizing, with movements such as restructuring and total quality management. In the 1990s, institutions were called on to make transformational change that transcends the institution as well as to redesign systems, working at a more macro level. Change models need to be aligned with types of change. Although there is currently little empirical support for this notion, it is an interesting concept to keep in mind. Do applicable change models vary with the changing political, social, and economic forces that affect higher education? A sociological view of higher education would suggest this might be true. Clark's work did not find such fluctuation, yet the sociological approach has not been fully tested. Could different approaches to change be successful in 2000, 2020, and 2030, depending on the overall societal landscape?

Another major area that is mostly unexplored is the impact on change of the increasing bureaucratization of universities. More institutions are being managed by administrators whose value systems focus on accountability, assessment, restructuring, privatization of services, and control. Furthermore, academic leadership through educational values is perceived as declining. What is the effect of bureaucratization and decline of academic leadership on change? There have been recent calls for responsive universities (Leslie and Fretwell, 1996; Keith, 1998) that react to increased expectations from external constituents, yet there is little research on institutions that have become responsive. What is the impact on the institution? How does it maintain consistency and sort out competing agendas? The entrepreneurial organization needs further analysis.

Another major area that is mostly unexplored is the impact on change of the increasing bureaucratization of universities.

To what degree might there be a garbage-can model of change in higher education, as there is for decision-making? It appears that researchers have stayed away from the ambiguity of the change process, instead favoring teleological, social-cognition, or evolutionary models in higher education. Birnbaum (1991) has been one of the only researchers to suggest that change should not be the norm in higher education and that the system should be allowed to work at homeostasis until a feedback loop illustrates a problem in need of attention. Even then, he characterizes change as problematic and tells leaders to try to examine the issue through as many lenses as possible, but to accept the realization that they have little direct control over creating change. We need a more detailed understanding of the ways in which change is elusive to planning, centralized decision-making, and strategy, if only to persuade individuals who see these as the key mechanisms that they may want to rethink their assumptions.

Although teleological models have not been applied with much success within higher education, there are some important areas that warrant further examination. Teleological models applied within other organizations have found that fostering individual and team learning is a facilitator of change. It seems that learning would be critical to change within higher education. Studies of sensemaking and the importance of developing a personal understanding of the change initiative also tap into learning. This is an area in need of empirical research, moving beyond the anecdotal support for learning organizations. There also needs to be more research on how teleological models can be successful within subunits of the institution, driven by administrative values and supported by more centralized structures. Also, as noted in the introduction to article five, we do not understand if working within the culture and structure of the academic enterprise always facilitates change to a greater degree than challenging this system. Are there situations in which the unique characteristics of higher education institutions facilitate or hinder change? Are there circumstances under which challenging the system facilitates or hinders change?

An important new direction for research is the application of life-cycle models to higher education. The ways in which staff development and training are used to facilitate individual and institutional identity development are in need of exploration. Also, to what degree does institutional identity change over the life cycle? Community colleges (as a newer institutional type) or the emerging virtual university sector might be interesting case studies for understanding the issues of identity related to change. Comparisons between colleges with long histories and those that are emerging might also prove interesting. Does one institutional type change with greater ease than another? Do certain institutions have life cycles in which change is more prevalent than do others? Does change take on a different character in different stages of the life cycle? These studies may prove helpful to institutions along the entire continuum of development, identifying key factors for their particular situations and enhancing our ability to construct context-based models.

Although we are aware that political processes shape change and we have gained some insight into how this process occurs, we know less about how politics overlap with other aspects of change. Do politics hinder or enable adaptability? How does the environment affect politics? How do politics influence organizational identity? As notions of power and politics are changing (such as feminist notions), how might politics be an enabler of equitable change? Another area in which we have a limited understanding is informal processes and how they operate; these are often noted in studies as key, but their nature is not carefully described. We also know very little about what motivates people to join in political turf wars. We know it is based on their interest, but this oversimplifies this complex process and the motivations of human beings. In any given situation involving two people, each with a vested political interest, what makes one persistent while another ignores the situation? I already noted that we need to better understand the growing managerialism; we also need to know how managerialism acts on the politics of change. The higher education environment is apparently becoming more politically charged, making these models even more important for future study.

The prominence of image and identity within some of the existing studies of change suggest this as an important line of research for further development. How does the relationship between identity and change affect individuals within institutions? Can regressive change be harmful to people whose identities are closely tied to the organization? Some change theories suggest that identification with the organization should be altered so that change can occur. What would be the result if this approach were taken in higher education? Do we want to make long-time committed employees identify less with their organization?

Imitation or emulation seems another important area for research. Theories about fashion or fads as an analogy for change help us understand the interest in new approaches to learning, teaching, or managing. However, in some situations this may prove challenging to study; as Clark (1983a) notes, changes creep across institutions quietly and with little notice. One line of research might help; Czarniawska and Sevon (1996) used new institutionalist theory, examining imitation among banks, railways, and local governments in Europe. Their research on imitation can serve as a model to better understanding these quiet and unnoticed processes.

We know very little about individual reactions to change in higher education, except perhaps in the area of technology adoption and cognitive frames. What is the impact of increasing environmental vulnerability on faculty? Will it also affect people entering the professoriate? How do individuals feel about change? Feelings and emotions relating to change have been studied through cultural models among other types of institutions and have provided interesting findings on institutional commitment, morale, and quality.

Cultural models are just emerging; this area is in need of research, especially because initial research has found a strong relationship between institutional culture and the particular change strategies that will be successful on a campus. However, these initial studies examined institutions as a whole. Considering that most change is occurring throughout the organization, future studies need to examine the impact of department, division, and school cultures on the change process. There also needs to be empirical research on whether there is a culture of change or certain cultures that are more open to change. The roles of attitudes, motivations, emotions, intuition, energy, enthusiasm, and other human dimensions need closer analysis. This seems like a particularly important area, as social-cognition studies have already illustrated the impact of mental models and embedded norms on resisting and facilitating change, which are concepts similar to attitudes and emotions. We also need more detailed studies of the effect of institutional type on the change process. There have been only cursory studies about the various institutional characteristics that might be related to change processes.

Lueddeke's proposed model (1999) needs to be empirically tested. It brings together many important principles from the research on higher education change. It best reflects the various propositions offered above, yet there are ways in which the model may need to be adjusted as it is tested. For example, existing research suggests that its linearity will need to be modified. How much generative learning actually occurs? What might be added to Lueddeke's model to develop a more comprehensive approach? For example, his model excludes all political assumptions related to change and maintains few assumptions from cultural models. Almost no higher education researcher has examined the various models as different aspects or levels of the change process. It would be helpful to compare how each type of model sheds light on change at the broadest level (evolutionary), life stage of the organization (life cycle), the intricacies of the organization (cultural), power and interest groups (political), and individual worldviews (social cognition).

Other, more general lines of research include the question of why some changes occur with relative ease, while others drag on for years. Levine (1978) proposes that compatibility and profitability are the two key factors determining why innovations succeed or fail. We need further research in this area, as there have been few extensive studies. What about the progressive nature of change? Can we document recent changes that were not progressive, but actually hurt a campus? What is the impact of regressive change? This may be a common type of change on campuses. Some historical analysis exists about higher education's response to the world wars. World War I had a regressive impact on campus; some scholars suggest that institutions learned from that experience and responded in more adaptive ways to the World War II (Lucas, 1994). Are there ways in which can we begin to understand more about current organizational learning and changes in response, as has been done in historical analysis? How can we reconcile the contradictions of loose coupling and institutional theory, which both seem to be such powerful forces in higher education institutions and on the change process? Can institutions as a whole drift without any (or much) intentional work, especially given the uncoordinated system? How do loose coupling and institutional theory interact? Some scholars have suggested that the new context of higher education requires change to be more macroscopic in nature and that interinstitutional alliances will be critical for creating change. Because little macro-level organizational change has occurred intentionally, this has been extremely difficult to study or understand. What does macro-level change look like? Is it possible, and if so, under what circumstances? How can institutional alliances facilitate sector or regional changes?

In terms of methodology, more long-term and context-based research is needed. There is an entire literature base on the complexities of studying change (Dawson, 1994; Gautam and others, 1997; Glick and others, 1990; Huber and Van de Ven, 1995; Monge, 1990; Pettigrew, 1985, 1987; Van de Ven and Poole, 1995). More researchers in higher education need to become familiar with this literature as they engage in studies. The few context-based studies have tended to examine one institution, and almost no research is multiyear. More studies in the tradition of Dawson (1994) and Pettigrew (1985) are needed. These researchers have studied change through ethnographic approaches over multiyear periods.

In closing, much research on organizational change needs to be conducted to help higher education institutions facilitate the process and maintain their traditions of excellence, even when the public and legislators demand unprecedented amounts of change. It is hoped that this synthesis of research-based principles and of areas needing more research will help serve as a blueprint for guiding research, policy, and practice in the next decade.

References

Albert, S., and Whetten, D. (1985). Organizational identity. *Research in Organizational Behavior, 7,* 263–295.

Alpert, D. (1991). Performance and paralysis: The organizational context of the American research university. In M. W. Peterson, E. E. Chaffee, and T. H. White (Eds.), *ASHE Reader on Organization and Governance in Higher Education* (4th ed.). Needham Heights, MA.: Ginn Press.

Alfred, R., and Carter, P. (1996). Inside track to the future: Structures, strategies, and leadership for change. *Community College Journal,* February–March, 10–19.

Alfred, R., and Carter, P. (1997). Out of the box: Strategies for building high performing colleges. *Community College Journal, 67*(5), 41–44.

Altbach, P., Berdhal, R., and Gumport, P. (Eds.) (1994). *American Higher Education in the 21st Century.* Amherst, NY: Prometheus Books.

Argyris, C. (1982). How learning and reasoning processes affect organizational change. In P. S. Goodman (Ed.), *Change in Organizations.* San Francisco: Jossey-Bass.

Argyris, C. (1994). *On Organizational Learning.* Oxford: Blackwell.

Astin, A. (1993). *What matters in college? Four critical years revisited.* San Francisco: Jossey-Bass.

Astin, H. S., and Leland, C. (1991). *Women of influence, women of vision: A cross generational study of leaders and social change.* San Francisco: Jossey-Bass.

Aune, B. P. (1995). The human dimension of organizational change. *Review of Higher Education, 18*(2), 149–173.

Austin, M. J. (1997). The peer support group needed to guide organizational change processes. *New Directions for Higher Education, 25*(2), 57–66.

Balderston, F. E. (1995). *Managing today's university: Strategies for viability, change and excellence* (2nd ed.). San Francisco: Jossey-Bass.

Baldridge, J. V. (1971). *Power and Conflict in the University.* New York: John Wiley.

Baldridge, J. V., Curtis, D. V., Ecker, G. P., and Riley, G. L. (1977). Alternative models of governance in higher education. In G. L. Riley and J. V. Baldridge (Eds.), *Governing Academic Organizations.* Berkeley: McCutchan.

Baldridge, J. V., and Deal, T. E. (1983). The basics of change in educational organizations. In J. V. Baldridge, T. E. Deal, and C. Ingols (Eds.), *The dynamics of Organizational Change in Education*. Berkeley: McCutchan.

Banta, T. W., and others (1996). Performance funding comes of age in Tennessee. *Journal of Higher Education, 67*(1), 23–45.

Barrow, C. W. (1996). The strategy of selective excellence: Redesigning higher education for global competition. *Higher Education, 31*(4).

Benjamin, M. (1996). *Cultural diversity, educational equity and the transformation of higher education: Group profiles as a guide to policy and programming.* Westport, CT: Praeger.

Benjamin, R., and Carroll, S. J. (1996). Impediments and imperatives in restructuring higher education. *Educational Administration Quarterly, 32*, 705–719.

Bensimon, E. M., and Neumann, A. (1993). *Redesigning Collegiate Leadership.* Baltimore: Johns Hopkins University Press.

Bensimon, E. M., Neumann, A., and Birnbaum, R. (1989). *Making sense of administrative leadership: The "L" word in higher education.* ASHE-ERIC Higher Education Report, no. 1. San Francisco: Jossey-Bass.

Berdhal, R. O. (1991). Shared governance and external constraints. In M. W. Peterson, E. E. Chaffee, and T. H. White (Eds.), *ASHE Reader on Organization and Governance in Higher Education* (4th ed.). Needham Heights, MA: Ginn Press.

Bergquist, W. (1992). *The four cultures of the academy: Insights and strategies for improving leadership in collegiate organizations.* San Francisco: Jossey-Bass.

Bergquist, W. (1998). The postmodern challenge: Changing our community colleges. In J. S. Levine (Ed.), *Organizational change in the community college: A ripple or a sea of change.* San Francisco: Jossey-Bass.

Bess, J. L. (1999). *The ambiguity of authority in colleges and universities: Why the new managerialism is winning.* Paper presented at the annual meeting of the Association for the Study of Higher Education, San Antonio, TX.

Birnbaum, R. (1991a). *How colleges work: The cybernetics of academic organization and leadership.* San Francisco: Jossey-Bass.

Birnbaum, R. (1991b). The latent functions of the academic senate: Why senates do not work but will not go away. In M. W. Peterson (Ed.), *ASHE Reader on Leadership and Governance.* Needham Heights, MA: Ginn Press.

Birnbaum, R. (2000). *Management Fads in Higher Education.* San Francisco: Jossey-Bass.

Blackburn, R., and Lawrence, J. (1995). *Faculty at work: Motivation, expectation, and satisfaction.* Baltimore: Johns Hopkins University Press.

Bolman, L. G., and Deal, T. E. (1991). *Reframing organizations: Artistry, choice, and leadership.* San Francisco: Jossey-Bass.

Bowen, H. ([1977] 1997). *Investment in Learning.* Baltimore: Johns Hopkins University Press.

Brill, P. L., and Worth, R. (1997). *The Four Levers of Corporate Change.* New York: American Management Association.

Brown, C. (2000). *ASHE Reader on Organization and Governance in Higher Education* (5th ed.). Boston: Pearson.

Brown, J. (1997). On becoming a learning organization. *About Campus, 1*(6), 5–10.

Brunner, I. (1997, March). *Accelerated schools as learning organizations: Cases from the University of New Orleans accelerated school network.* Paper presented at the annual meeting of the American Educational Research Association, Chicago, IL.

Burke, W. (1995). Organizational change: What we know, what we need to know. *Journal of Management Inquiry, 4*(2), 158–171.

Burnes, B. (1996). *Managing change: A strategic approach to organizational dynamics.* London: Pitman.

Burton, J. L. (1993). Hopping out of the swamp: Management of change in a downsizing environment. *Business Officer, 26*(8), 42–45.

Bushe, G. R., and, Shani, A. B. (1991). *Parallel learning structure: Increasing innovation in bureaucracies.* Reading, MA: Addison-Wesley.

Calas, M., and Smirich, L. (1992). Re-writing gender into organizational theorizing: Directions from feminist perspectives. In M. Reed and M. Hughes (Eds.), *Rethinking Organizations: New Directions in Organizational Theory and Analysis.* Beverly Hills: Sage.

Cameron, K. S. (1983). Strategic responses to conditions of decline: Higher education and the private sector. *Journal of Higher Education, 54*(4), 359–380.

Cameron, K. S. (1991). Organizational adaptation and higher education. In M. W. Peterson, E. E. Chaffee, and T. H. White (Eds.), *ASHE Reader on Organization and Governance in Higher Education* (4th ed.). Needham Heights, MA: Ginn Press.

Cameron, K. S., and Quinn, R. E. (1983). The field of organizational development. In R. E. Quinn and K. S. Cameron (Eds.), *Classics in Organizational Development.* Oak Park, IL: Moore.

Cameron, K. S., and Quinn, R. E. (1988). Organizational paradox and transformation. In K. S. Cameron and R. E. Quinn (Eds.), *Paradox and Transformation.* New York: Bellinger.

Cameron, K. S., and Smart, J. (1998). Maintaining effectiveness amid downsizing and decline in institutions of higher education. *Research in Higher Education, 39*(1), 65–86.

Cameron, K. S., and Tschichart, M. (1992). Post industrial environments and organizational effectiveness in colleges and universities. *Journal of Higher Education, 63*(1).

Cameron, K. S., and Whetten, D. (1983). Models of organizational life cycle. *Review of Higher Education, 6*(4).

Carlson-Dakes, C., and Sanders, K. (1998). *A movement approach to organizational change: Understanding the influences of a collaborative faculty development program.* Paper presented at the annual meeting of the Association for the Study of Higher Education, Miami, FL. (ED 427 591)

Carnall, C. A. (1995). *Managing Change in Organizations* (2nd ed.). London: Prentice Hall.

Carr, C. (1996). *Choice, chance, and organizational change: Practical insights from evolution for business leaders and thinkers.* New York: Amacom.

Carr, D., Hard, K., and Trahant, W. (1996). *Managing the change process: A field book for change agents, consultants, team leaders, and reengineering managers.* New York: McGraw-Hill.

Chaffee, E. (1983). Three models of strategy. *Academy of Management Review, 10*(1), 89–98.

Chaffee, E. (1991). The role of rationality in university budgeting. In M. W. Peterson (Ed.), *ASHE Reader on Leadership and Governance.* Needham Heights, MA: Ginn Press.

Chait, R. (1996). *The new activism of corporate boards and the implications for campus governance.* AGB Occasional Paper, no. 26. Washington, D.C.: Association of Governing Boards of Universities and Colleges.

Chance, W. (1995). Is taxonomy planning's biggest obstacle? *Planning for Higher Education, 23*(2), 1–4.

Chermak, G.L.D. (1990). Cultural dynamics: Principles to guide change in higher education. *CUPA Journal, 41*(3), 25–27.

Childers, M. E. (1981). What is political about bureaucratic-collegial decision-making? *Review of Higher Education, 5*(1), 25–45.

Clark, B. R. (1976). The benefits of disorder. *Change, 8*(9), 31–37. (EJ 146 825)

Clark, B. R. (1983a). *The higher education system: Academic organization in cross-national perspective.* Berkeley: University of California Press. (ED 262 687)

Clark, B. R. (1983b). The contradictions of change in academic systems. *Higher Education 12*(1), 101–116. (EJ 279 751).

Clark, B. R. (1991a). Faculty organization and authority. In M. W. Peterson (Ed.), *ASHE Reader on Leadership and Governance* (pp. 449–458). Needham Heights, MA: Ginn Press.

Clark, B. R. (1991b). The organizational saga in higher education. In M. W. Peterson (Ed.), *ASHE Reader on Leadership and Governance* (pp. 46–52). Needham Heights, MA: Ginn Press.

Clark, B. R. (1996a). Leadership and innovation in universities: From theory to practice. *Tertiary Education and Management, 1*(1), 7–11.

Clark, B. R. (1996b). Substantive growth and innovative organization: New categories for higher education research. *Higher Education, 32*(4), 417–420.

Clark, B. R. (1998). *Creating entrepreneurial universities: Organizational pathways of transformation.* Oxford: Pergamon Press.

Cohen, A. (1998). The Shaping of American Higher Education. San Francisco: Jossey-Bass.

Cohen, M. D., and March, J. G. (1974). *Leadership and ambiguity: The American college president.* Boston: Harvard Business School Press.

Cohen, M. D., and March, J. G. (1991a). Leadership in an organized anarchy. In M. W. Peterson, E. E. Chaffee, and T. H. White (Eds.), *ASHE Reader on Organization and Governance in Higher Education* (4th ed.). Needham Heights, MA: Ginn Press.

Cohen, M. D., and March, J. G. (1991b). The processes of choice. In M. W. Peterson, E. E. Chaffee, and T. H. White (Eds.), *ASHE Reader on Organization and Governance in Higher Education* (4th ed.). Needham Heights, MA: Ginn Press.

Collins, D. (1998). *Organizational change: Sociological perspectives.* London: Routledge.

Collins, V. H. (1996). *The faculty role in governance: A historical analysis of the influence of the American association of university professors and the middle states association on academic decision making.* ASHE annual meeting paper. (EJ 402 840)

Conrad, C. F. (1978). A grounded theory of academic change. *Sociology of Education 51*, 101–112.

Costello, D. E. (1994). Accreditation: Impact on faculty roles. *Metropolitan Universities: An International Forum, 5*(1), 68–70. (EJ 499 499)

Cowan, R. B. (1993). Prescription for small-college turnaround. *Change, 25*(1), 30–39.

Cox, T. (1993). *Cultural Diversity in Organizations.* San Francisco: Berrett-Koehler.

Curry, B. K. (1992). *Instituting enduring innovations: Achieving continuity of change in higher education.* ASHE-ERIC Higher Education Report, no. 7. Washington, D.C.: School of Education and Human Development, George Washington University.

Czarniawska, B., and Sevon, G. (1996). *Translating Organizational Change.* Berlin: Walter de Gruyter.

Daoud, A., and others (1996). Research and planning: Educating the campus community for institutional change and student success. *Metropolitan Universities: An International Forum, 7*(2), 41–50.

Davies, J. L. (1997). The evolution of university responses to financial reduction. *Higher Education Management, 9*(1), 127–140.

Dawson, P. (1994). *Organizational change: A processual approach.* London: Paul Chapman.

Dill, D. D. (1982). The management of academic culture: Notes on the management of meaning and social integration. *Higher Education, 11,* 303–320.

Dill, D. D., and Friedman, C. P. (1979). An analysis of frameworks for research on innovation and change in higher education. *Review of Education Research, 49*(3), 411–435.

Dill, D. D., and Helm, K. P. (1988). Faculty participation in policy making. In J. Smart (Ed.), *Higher education: Handbook of theory and research (vol. IV).* New York: Agathon.

DiMaggio, P. J., and Powell, W. W. (1983). The iron cage revisited: Institutional isomorphism and collective rationality in organizational fields. *American Sociological Review, 48,* 147–160.

Dominick, C. A. (1990). *Revising the institutional mission.* New Directions for Higher Education, no. 71. San Francisco: Jossey-Bass.

Donofrio, K. (1990). *Compensation Survey.* Washington, D.C.: College and University Personnel Association.

Drucker, P. (1990). *Managing Non-profit Organizations.* New York: HarperCollins.

Dufty, N. F. (1980). Are universities rational organizations? *Journal of Tertiary Educational Administration, 2*(1), 27–35.

Eckel, P. D. (1998). *How institutions discontinue academic programs: Making potentially adverse decisions in an environment of shared decision making.* Unpublished doctoral dissertation, University of Maryland, College Park.

Eckel, P., Hill, B., and Green, M. (1998). *En route to transformation.* On Change: Occasional Paper, no. 1. Washington, D.C.: American Council on Education.

Eckel, P., Hill, B., Green, M., and Mallon, B. (1999). *Taking charge of change: A primer for colleges and universities.* On Change: Occasional Paper, no. 3. Washington, D.C.: American Council on Education.

Eckel, P., and Kezar, A. (forthcoming). Strategies for making new institutional sense: Key ingredients to higher education transformation. *Review of Higher Education.*

Eckel, P., Kezar, A., and Lieberman (2000). Toward better-informed decisions: Reading groups as a campus tool. In A. Kezar and P. Eckel (Eds.), *Moving Beyond the Gap Between Research and Practice in Higher Education.* New Directions in Higher Education, no. 115. San Francisco: Jossey-Bass.

El-Khawas, E. (1995). External review: Alternative models based on U.S. experience. *Higher Education Management, 7*(1), 39–48.

El-Khawas, E. (2000). The impetus for organisational change: An exploration. *Tertiary Education and Management, 6,* 37–46.

Elliot, D. (1993). Overcoming institutional barriers to broad-based curricular change. *Innovative Higher Education, 18*(1), 37–46. (EJ 483 613)

Elton, L., and Cryer, P. (1994). Quality and change in higher education. *Innovative Higher Education, 18,* 205–220.

Farmer, D. (1990). Strategies for change. In D. Steeples (Ed.), *Managing Change in Higher Education.* New Directions for Higher Education, no. 71. San Francisco: Jossey-Bass.

Fear, F. (1994). *Initiating, implementing, and studying large scale university change: Outreach at Michigan State University.* (ED 377 749)

Feldman, M. S. (1991). The meanings of ambiguity: Learning from stories and metaphors. In P. J. Frost, and others (Eds.), *Reframing Organizational Culture.* Newbury Park, CA: Sage.

Finklestein, M., Seal, M., and Schuster, J. (1999). New entrants to the full-time faculty of higher education institutions. *Education Statistics Quarterly, 1*(4), 78–80.

Fletcher, B. R. (1990). *Organization transformation-theorists and practitioners: Profiles and themes.* New York: Praeger.

Freed, J., Klugman, M., and Fife, J. (1997). *A culture for academic excellence: Implementing quality principles in higher education.* Washington, D.C.: ASHE-ERIC Higher Education Report Series, 25-1.

Friere, P. (1999). *Pedagogy of the Oppressed.* New York: Continuum.

Frost, S. H., Gillespie, T. W. (1998). *Organizations, culture, and teams: Links toward genuine challenge.* New Directions for Institutional Research, no. 100. San Francisco: Jossey-Bass.

Gamson, Z. (1999, Spring). International Higher Education Newsletter.

Gardenswartz, L., and Rowe, A. (1994). *Diverse teams at work: Capitalizing on power of diversity.* Chicago: Irwin.

Gates, G. (1997). Isomorphism, homogeneity, and rationalism in university retrenchment. *Review of Higher Education, 20*(3), 253–275.

Gautam, K., and others (1997). Theoretical implications of measurement inconsistencies in organizational decline research. *Review of Higher Education, 20*(2), 181–198.

Gersick, C.J.G. (1991). Revolutionary change theories: A multilevel exploration of the punctuated equilibrium paradigm. *Academy of Management Review, 16*(1), 10–36.

Gioia, D. A., Thomas, J. B. (1996). Identity, image, and issue interpretation: Sensemaking during strategic change in academia. *Administrative Science Quarterly, 41,* 370–403.

Gioia, D. A., Thomas, J. B., Clark, S. M., and Chittipeddi, K. (1996). Symbolism and strategic change in academia: The dynamics of sensemaking and influence. In J. R. Meindl, C. Stubbart, and J. F. Poroc (Eds.), *Cognition in Groups and Organizations*. London: Sage.

Glick, W. H., and others (1990). Studying changes in organizational design and effectiveness: Retrospective event histories and periodic assessments. *Organizational Science, 1*(3), 293–312.

Golembiewski, R. T. (1989). *Ironies in Organizational Development*. London: Transaction.

Goodman, P. S. (1982). *Change in organizations: New perspectives on theory, research, and practice*. San Francisco: Jossey-Bass.

Green, M. F. (1997). Leadership and institutional change: A comparative view. *Higher Education Management, 9*(2), 135–146.

Green, M. F. (1998). *Change in higher education: It's not the same as in corporations*. Washington, D.C.: American Council on Education.

Green, M. F. (2000). Bridging the gap: Multiple players, multiple approaches. In A. Kezar and P. Eckel (Eds.), *Moving Beyond the Gap Between Research and Practice in Higher Education*. New Directions in Higher Education, no. 115. San Francisco: Jossey-Bass.

Green, M. F., and Hayward, F. (Eds.) (1997). *Transforming higher education: Views from the leaders around the world*. Phoenix, AZ: Oryx.

Greenwood, R., and Hinings, C. R. (2000). Understanding radical organizational change. In M. C. Brown II (Ed.), *ASHE Reader on Organization and Governance* (5th ed). New York: Pearson.

Gumport, P. J. (1993). Contested terrain of academic program reduction. *Journal of Higher Education, 64*(3), 283–311.

Gumport, P. J. (2000). *Academic governance: New light on old issues*. AGB Occasional Paper. Washington, D.C.: Association of Governing Boards of Universities and Colleges.

Gumport, P. J., and Pusser, B. (1995). A case of bureaucratic accretion: Context and consequences. *Journal of Higher Education, 66*(5), 493–520.

Gumport, P. J., and Pusser, B. (1999). University restructuring: The role of economic and political contexts. In J. Smart (Ed.), *Higher education: Handbook of theory and research (vol. XIV)*. New York: Agathon.

Gumport, P. J., and Sporn, B. (1999). Institutional adaptation: Demands for management reform and university administration. In J. Smart (Ed.), *Higher education: Handbook of theory and research (vol. XIV)*. New York: Agathon.

Guskin, A. E. (1994). *Reducing student costs and enhancing student learning*. AGB Occasional Paper, no. 27. Washington, D.C.: Association of Governing Boards of Universities and Colleges.

Guskin, A. E. (1996). Facing the future: The change process in restructuring universities. *Change, 28*(4), 27–37.

Guy, T. C., and others (1998). Infusing multicultural education: A process of creating organizational change at the college level. *Innovative Higher Education, 22*(4), 271–289.

Handy, C. (1994). *The Age of Paradox*. Boston: Harvard Business School Press.

Handy, C. (1995). *Beyond Certainty: The Changing Worlds of Organizations.* London: Hutchinson.

Harris, S. G. (1996). Organizational culture and individual sensemaking: A schema-based perspective. In J. R. Meindl, C. Stubbart, and J. F. Poroc (Eds.), *Cognition in Groups and Organizations.* London: Sage.

Hearn, J. C. (1996). Transforming U.S. higher education: An organizational perspective. *Innovative Higher Education, 21*(2), 141–154. (EJ 534 330)

Hearn, J. C., Clugston, R., and Heydinger, R. (1993). Five years of strategic environmental assessment efforts at a research university: A case study of an organizational innovation. *Innovative Higher Education, 18*(1), 7–36.

Hedberg, B. (1981). How organizations learn and unlearn. In P. C. Nystrom and W. H. Starbuck (Eds.), *Handbook of Organizational Design.* New York: Oxford University Press.

Heydinger, R. (1997). Principles of redesigning organizations. In M. Peterson, D. Dill, and L. Mets (Eds.), *Planning and Management.* San Francisco: Jossey-Bass.

Higher Education Research Institute (1995). *A Social Change Model of Leadership.* Los Angeles: Higher Education Research Institute.

Houghton, J., and Jurick, D. M. (1995). Redesigning the university: The process of self-study. *Liberal Education, 81*(2), 44–49.

Hrebiniak, L. G., and Joyce, W. F. (1985). Organizational adaptation: Strategic choice and environmental determinism. *Administrative Science Quarterly, 30,* 336–349.

Huber, G. P., and Glick, W. H. (1993). *Organizational change and redesign: Ideas and insights for improving performance.* New York: Oxford University Press.

Huber, G. P., and Van de Ven, A. H. (Eds.) (1995). *Longitudinal field research methods: Studying processes of organizational change.* Thousand Oaks, CA: Sage.

Hyatt, J. A. (1993). *Strategic restructuring: A case study.* New Directions for Higher Education, no. 82. San Francisco: Jossey-Bass.

Johnstone, D., Dye, B., and Johnson, R. (1998). Collaborative Leadership for Institutional Change. *Liberal Education, 84*(2), 12–19.

Kaiser, J. R., and Kaiser, P. R. (1994). Persuasive messages to support planned change. *College and University, 69*(2), 124–129.

Kanter, R. (1983). *The Change Masters.* New York: Simon & Schuster.

Kanter, R. (1998). Three tiers for innovation research. *Communication-Research, 15*(5), 509–523. (EJ 379 891)

Kanter, R. (2000). *Evolve: Succeeding in the digital culture tomorrow.* Boston: Harvard Business School Press.

Keith, K. M. (1998). The responsive university in the twenty-first century. In W. G. Tierney (Ed.), *The responsive university: Restructuring for high performance.* Baltimore: Johns Hopkins University Press.

Keller, G. (1983). Shaping an academic strategy. In G. Keller (Ed.), *Academic strategy: The management revolution in American higher education.* Baltimore: Johns Hopkins University Press.

Keller, G. (1997). Examining what works in strategic planning. In M. W. Peterson, D. D. Dill, and L. A. Mets (Eds.), *Planning and management for a changing environment: A handbook in redesigning postsecondary institutions.* San Francisco: Jossey-Bass.

Kelly, M. (1998). Enabling metaphors of innovation and change. In J. Meyerson (Ed.), *New Thinking on Higher Education.* Bolton, MA: Anker.

Kerka, S. (1995). *The learning organization: Myths and realities.* (ED 388 802)

Kerr, C. (1984). *Presidents make a difference: Strengthening leadership in colleges and universities.* Washington, D.C.: Association of Governing Boards of Universities and Colleges.

Kerr, C., and Gade, M. (1986). *The Many Lives of Academic Presidents.* Washington, D.C.: Association of Governing Boards of Universities and Colleges.

Kezar, A. (2000a). ERIC Trends. Washington, D.C.: ERIC Clearinghouse on Higher Edcuation. [www.eriche.org].

Kezar, A. (2000b). Higher Education research at the millennium: Still trees without fruit? *Review of Higher Education, 23*(4), 443–468.

Kezar, A., and Eckel, P. (forthcoming). Change strategies in higher education: Universal principles or culturally sensitive concepts? *Journal of Higher Education.*

Kezar, A., and Eckel, P. (forthcoming). Examining the institutional transformation process: The importance of sensemaking and inter-related strategies. *Research in Higher Education.*

Kezar, A., and El-Khawas, E. (forthcoming). Using the performance dimension: Converging paths for external accountability? In H. Eggins (Ed.), *Higher Education Reform.* London: Society for Research into Higher Education.

Kieser, A. (1989). Organizational, institutional and societal evolution: Medieval craft guilds and the genesis of formal organizations. *Administrative Science Quarterly, 34,* 540–564.

King, N., and Anderson, N. (1995). *Innovation and Change in Organizations.* London: Routledge.

Kliewer, J. R. (1999). *The innovative campus: Nurturing the distinctive learning environment.* Phoenix, AZ: Oryx.

Kotler, P., and Murphy, P. (1991). Strategic planning for higher education. In M. W. Peterson (Ed.), *ASHE Reader on Leadership and Governance.* Needham Heights, MA: Ginn Press.

Kotter, J. (1985). *Power and influence: Beyond formal authority.* New York: Free Press.

Kotter, J. (1996). *Leading Change.* Boston: Harvard Business School Press.

Leslie, D. W., and Fretwell, E. K., Jr. (1996). *Wise moves in hard times: Creating and managing resilient colleges and universities* (pp. 217–243). San Francisco: Jossey-Bass.

Levin, J. S. (1996). Limits to organizational change in the community college. *Community College Journal of Research and Practice, 20*(2), 185–197.

Levin, J. S. (1998a). Making sense of organizational change. In J. S. Levin (Ed.), *Organizational change in the community college: A ripple or a sea of change.* San Francisco: Jossey-Bass.

Levin, J. S. (1998b). Organizational change and the community college. In J. S. Levin (Ed.), *Organizational change in the community college: A ripple or a sea of change.* San Francisco: Jossey-Bass.

Levine, A. (1978). *The life and death of innovation in higher education*. Occasional Paper, no. 2. Buffalo, NY: Department of Higher Education, State University of New York. (ED 167 034)

Levine, A. (1980). *Why innovation fails: The institutionalization and termination of innovation in higher education*. Albany, NY: State University of New York.

Levy, A., and Merry, U. (1986). *Organizational transformation: Approaches, strategies, theories*. New York: Praeger.

Lindquist, J. (1978). *Strategies for Change*. Washington, D.C.: Council for Independent Colleges.

Lippitt, G. (1969). *Organizational renewal: Achieving viability in a changing world*. New York: Appleton-Century-Crofts.

London, M. (1995). *Achieving performance excellence in university administration: A team approach to organizational change and employee development*. Westport, CT: Praeger.

Love, P. G. (1997). Contradiction and paradox: Attempting to change the culture of sexual orientation at a small catholic college. *Review of Higher Education, 20*(4), 381–398.

Lovett, C. (1996). How to start restructuring our colleges. *Planning for Higher Education, 24*(3), 18–22.

Lovett, C. (1993). To affect intimately the lives of the people: American professors and their society. *Change, 25*(4), 26–37.

Lucas, C. (1994). *American higher education: A history*. New York: St. Martin's Press.

Lucas, A. F., and Assoc. (2000). *Leading academic change: Essential roles for department chairs*. San Francisco: Jossey-Bass.

Lueddeke, G. R. (1999). Toward a constructivist framework for guiding change and innovation in higher education. *Journal of Higher Education, 70*(3), 235–260.

Lyons, P. (1999). *Assessment techniques to enhance organizational learning*. (ED 426 678)

MacDonald, J. (1997). *Calling a halt to mindless change: A plea for commonsense management*. New York: American Management Association.

MacTaggart, T. (1996). Restructuring and the failure of reform. In T. MacTaggart (Ed.), *Restructuring Higher Education*. San Francisco: Jossey-Bass.

March, J. G. (1981). Footnotes to organizational change. *Administrative Science Quarterly, 26*, 563–577.

March, J. G. (1991). Exploration and exploitation in organizational learning. *Organizational Science, 2*(1), 71–87.

March, J. G. (1994a). The evolution of evolution. In J.A.C. Baum and J. V. Singh (Eds.), *Evolutionary Dynamics of Organizations*. New York: Cambridge University Press.

March, J. G. (1994b). *A primer on decision making: How decisions happen*. New York: Free Press.

Martin, J. (1992). *Cultures in organizations: Three perspectives*. New York: Oxford University Press.

Mathews, K. (1990). Revising the institutional mission. In D. Steeples (Ed.), *Managing Change in Higher Education*. New Directions for Higher Education, no. 71. San Francisco: Jossey-Bass.

McMahon, J., and Caret, R. (1997). Redesigning the faculty roles and rewards structure. *Metropolitan Universities, 7*(4), 11–22.

McWhinney, W. (1992). *Paths of change: Strategic choices for organizations and society.* Newbury Park, CA: Sage.

Meek, V. L. (1990). The rise and fall of the binary policy of higher education in Australia. *Journal of Education Policy, 50*(3), 282–292.

Meek, V. L. (1991). The transformation of Australian higher education from binary to unitary system. *Higher Education, 21*(4), 461–494.

Mellow, G. O. (1996, October). *The role of the community college chair in organizational change: Chaos, leadership and the challenge of complexity.* Paper presented at the 2nd Annual Mid-Atlantic Community College Chair/Dean Conference Blue Bell, PA.

Meyer, A., Brooks, G., and Goes, J. (1990). Environmental jolts and industry revolutions: Organizational responses to discontinuous change. *Strategic Management Journal, 11,* 93–110.

Meyer, J., and Rowan, B. (1977). Institutionalizing organization. *American Journal of Sociology, 83*(2).

Meyerson, J. W. (1998). *New thinking on higher education: Creating a context for change.* Bolton, MA: Anker.

Millar, S. (1993). *Monological Innovation versus Polylogical Improvement.* State College, PA: Pennsylvania State University.

Miller, D., and Friesen, P. (1980). Archetypes of organizational transition. *Administrative Science Quarterly, 25*(2), 268–299.

Miller, H. (1995). *The management of change in universities: Universities, state and economy in Australia, Canada and the United Kingdom.* Buckingham, U.K.: Society for Research into Higher Education and Open University Press.

Miller, R. (1999). *Major American higher education issues and challenges in the 21st century.* London: Jessica Kingsley.

Mintzberg, H. (1994). *Rise and Fall of Strategic Planning* New York: Free Press

Mintzberg, H. (2000). *Mastering Strategy.* Englewood Cliffs: Prentice Hall.

Morgan, G. (1986). *Images of Organization.* Newbury Park, CA: Sage.

Morgan, G. (1997). *Imaginization.* San Francisco: Berrett-Koehler.

Morphew, C. C. (1997). *Understanding the acquisition of new degree programs.* ASHE Annual Meeting Paper. (ED 415 801)

Morris, E.E.J. (1994). The four Rs of higher education: Restructure, reinvent, rightsize, revenue. *Business Officer, 28*(4), 45–47.

Nedwek, B. P. (1998). Organizational transformation begins with you. *Planning for Higher Education, 26*(4), 31–36.

Neumann, A. (1993). College planning: A cultural perspective. *Journal of Higher Education Management, 8*(2), 31–41.

Nevis, E. C., Lancourt, J., and Vassallo, H. G. (1996). *Intentional revolutions: A seven-point strategy for transforming organizations* (pp. 29–31). San Francisco: Jossey-Bass.

Newcombe, J. P., and Conrad, C. F. (1981). A theory of mandated academic change. *Journal of Higher Education, 52*(6), 555–557.

Nordvall, R. C. (1982). *The process of change in higher education institutions.* Washington, D.C.: American Association of Higher Education.

Norris, D. M., and Morrison, J. L. (1997). *Mobilizing for transformation: How campuses are preparing for the knowledge age.* New Directions for Institutional Research, no. 94. San Francisco: Jossey-Bass.

O'Toole, J. (1999). *Leading change: The argument for value based leadership.* Boston: Ballatine Press.

Parilla, R. E. (1993). *Adapting institutional structure and culture to change.* New Directions for Community Colleges, no. 21. San Francisco: Jossey-Bass.

Peters, T. (1987). *Thriving on Chaos.* New York: Harper & Row.

Peterson, M. W. (1995). Images of university structure, governance, and leadership: Adaptive strategies for the new environment. In D. D. Dill and B. Sporn (Eds.), *Emerging patterns of social demand and university reform: Through a glass darkly.* Oxford: Pergamon Press.

Peterson, M. W. (1997). Using contextual planning to transform institutions. In M. W. Peterson, D. D. Dill, and L. A. Mets (Eds.), *Planning and management for a changing environment.* San Francisco: Jossey-Bass.

Peterson, M. W. (Ed.) (1986). *ASHE Reader on Organization and Governance in Higher Education* (3rd ed.). Needham Heights, MA: Ginn Press.

Peterson, M. W., Dill, D. D., and Mets, L. A. (1997). *Planning and management for a changing environment: A handbook on redesigning postsecondary institutions.* San Francisco: Jossey-Bass.

Pettigrew, A. (1985). *Awakening giant: Continuity and change in ICI.* Oxford: Blackwell.

Pettigrew, A. (1987). Context and action in the transformation of the firm. *Journal of Management Studies, 24*(6), 649–670.

Phillips, R., and Duran, C. (1992). Effecting strategic change: Biological analogues and emerging organizational structures. In R. L. Phillips and J. G. Hunt (Eds.), *Strategic leadership: A multiorganizational-level perspective.* Westport, CT: Quorum.

Premeaux, S. R., and Mondy, R. W. (1996). Tenure: Administrative versus faculty perspectives. *CUPA Journal, 47*(1), 25–31.

Quinn, R., Kahn, J., and Mandle, M. (1994). Perspective on organizational behavior. In R. Greenberg (Ed.), *Organizational Behavior.* Hillsdale, NJ: Erlbaum.

Rajagopalan, N., and Spreitzer, G. M. (1996). Toward a theory of strategic change: A multi-lens perspective and integrated framework. *Academy of Management Review, 22*(1), 48–79.

Rhoades, G. (1995). Rethinking and restructuring universities. *Journal of Higher Education Management, 10*(2), 17–23.

Rhoades, G. (1998). *Managed professionals: Unionized faculty and restructuring academic labor.* Albany: State University of New York Press.

Rhoades, G., and Slaughter, S. (1997). Academic capitalism, managed professionals, and supply-side higher education. *Social Text, 15*(2), 11–38.

Rieley, J. (1997). *Reframing Organizational Thinking*. New York: Basic Books.

Roberts, A. O., Wergin, J. F., and Adam, B. E. (1993). *Institutional approaches to the issues of reward and scholarship*. New Directions for Higher Education, no. 81. San Francisco: Jossey-Bass.

Rogers, E. (1995). *Diffusion of Innovations*. New York: Free Press.

Rudolph, F. (1962). *The American college and university: A history*. Athens: University of Georgia Press.

Rubin, I. (1979). Retrenchment, loose structure, and adaptability in the university. *Sociology of Education, 52,* 211–222.

St. John, E. P. (1991). The transformation of private liberal arts colleges. *Review of Higher Education, 15*(1), 83–106.

Salanick, G., and Pfefferm, K. (1974). The bases and use of power in organizational decision making: The case of a university. *Administrative Science Quarterly, 19,* 453–473.

Salipante, P. (1992). Providing continuity in change: The role of tradition in long-term adaptation. In S. Srivastva, R. Fry, and Associates (Eds.), *Executive and organizational continuity: Managing the paradoxes of stability and change*. San Francisco: Jossey-Bass.

Salipante, P., and Golden-Biddle, K. (1995). Managing traditionality and strategic change in nonprofit organizations. *Nonprofit Management and Leadership, 6*(1), 3–19.

Schein, E. (1985). *Organizational culture and leadership: A dynamic view*. San Francisco: Jossey-Bass.

Scott, R. (1992). *Organizations: Rational, natural and open systems* (3rd ed.). Englewood Cliffs, NJ: Prentice Hall.

Scott, R. (1995). *Institutions and Organizations*. London: Sage.

Scott, W. (1987). The adolescence of institutional theory. *Administrative Science Quarterly,* 323.

Senge, P. (1990). *The fifth discipline: The art and practice of the learning organization*. New York: Doubleday.

Shaw, K. A., and Lee, K. E. (1997). Effecting change at Syracuse University: The importance of values, missions, and vision. *Metropolitan Universities: An International Forum, 7*(4), 23–30.

Simsek, H. (1997a). Metaphorical images of an organization: The power of symbolic constructs in reading change in higher education organizations. *Higher Education, 33*(3), 283–307.

Simsek, H. (1997b). Paradigm shift and strategic planning: Planning and management in a turbulent decade. *Educational Planning, 10*(3), 21–35.

Simsek, H., and Louis, K. S. (1994). Organizational change as paradigm shift: Analysis of the change process in a large, public university. *Journal of Higher Education, 65*(6), 670–695.

Sjostrand, S. (1993). On institutional thought in the social and economic sciences. In S. Sjostrand (Ed.), *Institutional change: Theory and empirical findings*. Armonk, NY: Sharpe.

Slowey, M. (Ed.) (1995). *Implementing change from within universities and colleges: Ten personal accounts*. London: Kogan Page.

Smart, J. C., Kuh, G., and Tierney, W. (1997). The roles of institutional cultures and decision approaches in promoting organizational effectiveness of the two-year college. *Journal of Higher Education, 68*(3), 256–282. (EJ 546 173)

Smart, J. C., and St. John, E. P. (1996). Organizational culture and effectiveness in higher education: A test of the "culture type" and "strong culture" hypothesis. *Educational Evaluation and Policy Analysis, 18*(3), 219–241.

Smirich, L. (1983). Organizations as shared meanings. In L. R. Pondy, P. J. Frost, G. Morgan, and T. C. Dandridge (Eds.), *Organizational Symbolism*. Greenwich, CT: JAI Press.

Smirich, L., and Calas, M. (1982). Organizational culture: A critical assessment. In M. W. Peterson (Ed.), *ASHE Reader on Organization and Governance in Higher Education*. Needham Heights, MA: Ginn Press.

Smith, D. T. (1993). The new view of biological evolution: Organizational applications to higher education. *Review of Higher Education, 12*(2), 141–156.

Sporn, B. (1999). *Adaptive university structures: An analysis of adaptation to socioeconomic environments of U.S. and European universities*. London: Jessica Kingsley.

Staw, B. (1976). Knee deep in the big muddy: A study of escalating commitment to a chosen action. *Organizational Behavior and Human Performance, 16*, 27–44.

Steeples, D. (1990). *Managing change in higher education*. New Directions for Higher Education, no. 71. San Francisco: Jossey-Bass.

Swenk, J. (1998). *Strategic planning and fiscal benefits: Is there a link?* Paper presented at the Annual Meeting of the Association for the Study of Higher Education, Miami, FL.

Taylor, A. L., and Karr, S. (1999). Strategic planning approaches used to respond to issues confronting research universities. *Innovative Higher Education, 23*(3), 221–234.

Taylor, A. L., and Koch, A. M. (1996). *The cultural context for effective strategy.* New Directions for Higher Education, no. 94. San Francisco: Jossey-Bass.

Teitel, L. (1991). The transformation of a community college. *Community College Review, 19*(1), 7–13.

Thor, L., Scarafiotti, C., and Helminshi, A. (1998). Managing change: A case study of evolving strategic management. In J. Levin (Ed.), *Organizational change in community colleges: A ripple or sea change?* New Directions for Community Colleges, no. 102. San Francisco: Jossey-Bass.

Thomas, J., and McDaniel, R. (1990). Interpreting strategic issues: Effects of strategy and the information processing structure of top management. *Academy of Management Journal, 33*, 286–306.

Thomas, J. B., Clark, S., and Gioia, D. A. (1993). Strategic sensemaking and organizational performance: Linkages among scanning, interpretation, action and outcomes. *Academy of Management Journal, 36*, 239–270.

Tierney, W. (1988). Organizational culture in higher education. *Journal of Higher Education, 59*, 2–21.

Tierney, W. (1991). Organizational culture in higher education: Defining the essentials. In M. W. Peterson (Ed.), *ASHE Reader on Organization and Governance in Higher Education.* Needham Heights, MA: Ginn Press.

Tierney, W., and Rhoades, R. (1993). *Enhancing promotion, tenure, and beyond: Faculty socialization as a cultural process.* Washington, D.C.: ASHE-ERIC Higher Education Report Series, 22-6.

Townsend, B. K., and Twombly, S. B. (1998). A feminist critique of organizational change in the community college. In J. S. Levin (Ed.), *Organizational change in the community college: A ripple or a sea of change.* San Francisco: Jossey-Bass.

Trow, M. (1993). Managerialism and the academic profession: The case of england. *Studies of Higher Education and Research,* 1–23.

Tushman, M. L., Newman, W. H., and Romanelli, E. (1986). Convergence and upheaval: Managing the unsteady pace of organizational evolution. *California Management Review, 29*(1), 29–44.

Van de Ven, A. H., and Poole, M. S. (1995). Explaining development and change in organizations. *Academy of Management Review, 20*(3), 510–540.

Walker, D. E. (1979). University administration on a political model. *Educational Record, 60*(3), 234–240.

Weick, K. E. (1979). *The Social Psychology of Organizing* (2nd ed.). New York: McGraw-Hill.

Weick, K. E. (1991). Educational organizations as loosely coupled systems. In M. W. Peterson, E. E. Chaffee, and T. H. White (Eds.), *Organization and Governance in Higher Education.* (4th ed.). Needham Heights, MA: Ginn Press.

Weick, K. E. (1993). The collapse of sensemaking in organizations: The Mann Gulch disaster. *Administrative Science Quarterly, 38*(4), 628–642.

Weick, K. E. (1995). *Sensemaking in Organizations.* Thousand Oaks, CA: Sage.

Weil, S. (Ed.) (1994). *Introducing change from the top in universities and colleges: Ten personal accounts* (pp. 83–85). London: Kogan Page.

Wheatley, M. J. (1999). *Leadership and the new science: Discovering order in a chaotic world* (2nd ed.). San Francisco: Berrett-Koehler.

Winston, G. (1998). Creating the context for change. In J. Meyerson (Ed.), *New Thinking on Higher Education* (pp. 1–14). Bolton, MA: Anker.

Wolverton, M., and others (1998). The department as a double agent: The call for department change and renewal. *Innovative Higher Education, 22*(3), 203–215.

Name Index

A

Adam, B. E., 90
Alfred, R., 87
Alpert, D., 62, 63
Altbach, P., 4
Anderson, N., 14
Argyis, C., 16, 21, 44, 45, 46, 100, 101, 109
Astin, A., 75, 76
Astin, H. S., 42, 68
Aune, B. P., 93
Austin, M. J., 93, 100

B

Balderston, F. E., 87
Baldridge, J. V., 41, 44, 72, 73, 84, 94, 96, 97, 98
Banta, T. W., 71, 75
Barrow, C. W., 34
Benjamin, M., 41, 105, 108
Benjamin, R., 87, 91
Bensimon, E. M., 42, 89, 101
Berdhal, R., 4
Berdhal, R. O., 5, 62, 63, 64, 118
Bergquist, W., 1, 2, 5, 18, 19, 41, 61, 65, 66, 73, 107, 108, 115, 117
Bess, J. L., 69, 75, 86, 90, 91
Birnbaum, R., vi, 1, 3, 5, 61, 63, 65, 66, 67, 68, 69, 71, 72, 73, 76, 82, 86, 88, 89, 90, 91, 101, 105, 106, 107, 109, 110, 119, 121, 128
Blackburn, R., 90

Bolman, L. G., v, 3, 37, 39, 41, 42, 47, 49, 54, 65, 102, 106, 121, 122
Bowen, H., 74–75
Brill, P. L., 33
Brooks, G., 18
Brown, J., 101, 109
Brunner, I., 101
Burke, W., 22
Burnes, B., iii, iv, 12, 14, 15, 17, 28, 31, 32, 36, 37, 40, 53, 55
Burton, J. L., 91
Bushe, G. R., 45

C

Calas, M., 43, 68
Cameron, K. S., 1, 14, 29, 31, 38, 51, 76, 81, 82, 83, 84, 88, 92
Caret, R., 90
Carnall, C. A., v, 15, 33
Carr, C., 108
Carr, D., v, 21, 33
Carroll, S. J., 87, 91
Carter, P., 87
Chaffee, E., 52, 81, 82, 83, 88, 91, 106
Chair, R, 80
Chermak, G.L.D., 107, 109
Childers, M. E., 96
Chittipeddi, K., 102, 103, 106
Clark, B. R., 5, 61, 67, 68, 69, 71, 81, 82, 85, 86, 89, 94, 95, 96, 98, 105, 106, 108, 114, 117, 119, 120, 125, 126, 127, 130
Clark, S., 102

Clark, S. M., 102, 103, 106
Cohen, A., 62, 64
Cohen, M. D., vii, 27, 47, 74, 75, 89, 97, 98, 105, 106, 108
Collins, D., 3, 28, 32, 36, 37, 45, 52, 53, 112
Collins, V. H., 73
Conrad, C. F., vii, 94, 96, 98
Costello, D. E., 62
Cowan, R. B., 89, 90
Cryer, P., 87
Curry, B. K., 13, 89
Curtis, D. V., 41, 44, 72, 73, 84, 94, 96, 97, 98
Czarniawska, B., 8, 27, 40, 66, 105, 130

D
Daoud, A., 88
Davies, J. L., 84
Dawson, P., 22, 51, 132
Deal, T. E., v, 3, 37, 39, 41, 42, 47, 49, 54, 65, 96, 98, 102, 106, 121, 122
Dill, D. D., 26, 106, 107
DiMaggio, P. J., 104
Dominick, C. A., 87
Donofrio, K., 74
Drucker, P., 60
Dufty, N. F., 35
Duran, C., 26, 27, 32
Dye, B., 73

E
Eckel, P., vii, 22, 84, 85, 87, 88, 89, 90, 100, 101, 102, 103, 106, 107, 108, 115, 117
Ecker, G. P., 41, 44, 72, 73, 84, 94, 96, 97, 98
El-Khawas, E., 62, 63, 82
Elton, L., 87

F
Farmer, D., 87, 89, 93
Feldman, M. S., 50
Fife, J., 34, 35, 91
Finklestein, M., 74
Freed, J., 34, 35, 91

Fretwell, E. K., Jr., 1, 5, 127
Friere, P., 116
Friesen, P., 36, 37
Frost, S. H., 109

G
Gade, M., 89, 112
Gamson, Z., 9
Gardenswartz, L., 90
Gates, G., 104
Gautam, K., 132
Gersick, C.J.G., 17
Gillespie, T. W., 109
Gioia, D. A., 75, 76, 85, 91, 92, 93, 94, 96, 97, 98, 100, 101, 102, 103, 104, 105, 106, 116
Glick, W. H., 33, 132
Goes, J., 18
Golden-Biddle, K., 26, 60, 61
Golembiewski, R. T., 33
Goodman, P.S., iv, 14, 16, 18, 22, 30, 33, 37, 92
Gould, ??, 17
Green, M., 22, 87, 88, 89, 90, 108, 117
Green, M. F., 1, 5, 59, 63
Greenwood, R., 104, 105
Gumport, P., 4
Gumport, P. J., 72, 80, 81, 82, 83, 84, 94, 95, 127
Guskin, A. E., 34

H
Handy, C., 60
Hard, K., v, 21, 33
Harris, S. G., 45, 46
Hayward, F., 1, 5
Hearn, J. C., vii, 70, 74, 76, 94, 97, 98, 111, 113
Hedberg, B., 45, 46
Helm, K. P., 26
Helminshi, A., 113
Hill, B., 22, 87, 88, 89, 90, 108, 117
Hinings, C. R., 104, 105
Houghton, J., 99
Hrebiniak, L. G., 28
Huber, G. P., 22, 33, 132

Prigogine, ??, 17
Pusser, B., 80, 81, 82, 83, 84, 94, 95

Q
Quinn, R. E., 84, 88

R
Rajagopalan, N., iv, 14, 15, 37, 53
Rhoades, G., 42, 72, 81, 83, 84, 95
Rhoads, R., 90
Rieley, J., 101
Riley, G. L., 41, 44, 72, 73, 84, 94, 96, 97, 98
Roberts, A. O., 90
Rogers, E., 13
Romanelli, E., 17
Rowe, A., 90
Rubin, I., 81

S
Salipante, P., 26, 60, 61
Scarafiotti, C., 113
Schein, E., v, 22, 36, 50, 51, 53, 109
Schuster, J., 74
Scott, R., 44, 104
Seal, M., 74
Senge, P., 19, 20, 21, 36, 40, 54, 55, 100, 101, 109, 112
Sevon, G., 8, 27, 40, 66, 105, 130
Shani, A. B., 45
Simsek, H., 94, 102, 107–108
Slaughter, S., 81, 83, 84
Slowey, M., 87
Smart, J. C., 66, 85, 107
Smirich, L., 43, 50, 68, 102
Smith, D. T., 81
Sporn, B., 5, 29, 30, 32, 61, 72, 80, 81, 82, 83, 85, 86, 94, 105, 108, 120

Spreitzer, G. M., iv, 14, 15, 37, 53
St. John, E. P., 66, 81, 84, 85, 88, 92
Staw, B., 109
Steeples, D., 21
Stengers, ??, 17
Swenk, J., 89

T
Taylor, A. L., 88, 89, 90, 109
Thomas, J. B., 75, 76, 85, 91, 92, 93, 94, 96, 97, 98, 100, 101, 102, 103, 104, 105, 106, 116
Thor, L., 113
Tierney, W., 85, 90, 106, 107
Townsend, B. K., 43
Trahant, W., v, 21, 33
Tschichart, M., 1, 83
Tushman, M. L., 17
Twombly, S. B., 43

V
Van de Ven, A. H., iii, v, 5, 12, 17, 22, 26, 36, 37, 38, 40, 53, 132
Vassallo, H. G., 49, 87

W
Walker, D. E., 96
Weick, K. E., vii, 5, 21, 44, 47, 48, 70, 99, 100, 101, 102, 126
Weil, S., 4
Wergin, J. F., 90
Wheatley, M. J., 31, 60, 115
Whetten, D., 76, 92
Winston, G., 59
Wolverton, M., 4
Worth, R., 33

Subject Index

A

Academic authority, 69

Accountability: as force of change, 1; as institutional goal, 62; new structures, 61; professionals and, 72–73

Accreditation, 62, 63

Accretion: evolutionary models and, vii, 81–82; future research and, 127; master plans and, 125

ACE Kellogg study, 108

Active change, iv, 21–22

Adaptation: in evolutionary models, 14; focus on, 126; master plans and, 125; as principle of change, 117; scale of change and, 18; as social evolutionary model, 28

Adaptive change: as concept, iv; dichotomies, 27; examined, 20

Adaptive learning (teleological models), 32

Adaptive University Structures (Sporn), 80

Administrative values, 72–73, 109

Adoption phase (diffusion model), 13

AGD-M (adaptive-generative development model), 110–111, 122

Alliance-building. *See* Coalition-building

Ambiguity: change and, 119; in change process, 127–128; cultural models and, 108; frustration with, 112; in goals, 74–75; organized anarchy and, 71; sensemaking and, 102; social-cognition models and, 99; teleological models and, 91

American Association for Higher Education, 62, 63, 120

American Council on Education, 62

Americorp, 63

Anarchies, higher education and organized, 71–72

Assessment: change at macro level, 25; cybernetic model and, 110; as force of change, 1; laying groundwork, 116–117; teleological models key concept, 33

Assumptions: about change, 25; in cultural models, 50; in dialectical models, 40–41; in evolutionary models, 28–30; life-cycle models, 36–37; models sharing, 28; in social-cognition models, 44–46; in teleological models, 32–33; theories of change models and, iv; of TQM, 34

Attitudes: as focus of change, 19; teleological models and, 33

Authority. *See* Power and authority structures

Autonomy: higher education and, 63–64; principle of, 9

Awareness phase (diffusion model), 13

B

Belief systems. *See* Values

Benefits: of cultural models, 52–53; of dialectical models, 43–44; of evolutionary models, 31–32; of life-cycle models, 39–40; models compared, 57–58; of social-cognition models, 48–49; of teleological models, 35–36

Bergquist (organizational cultures), 65

Biological models, 28

Bureaucratization, research on, 127

C

Calling a Halt to Mindless Change (MacDonald), 9

Cameron life-cycle model, 38

Campus Compact, 63, 120

Carnegie Classification System, 76

Catalysts for change in dialectical models, 95

Cause maps (cognition and change), 45

Change: characteristics of, vii; complexities of studying, 132; degree of, iv, 16–17; as mutation, 28; nature of, 131; as problematic, 128; as return to traditional values, 13; skills needed to create, 42; theories of, iv–v; types of, 127

Change agents: building coalitions, 42; change process and, 4; teleological models and, 34–35

Change initiatives: dialectical models and, 42; teleological models and, 33; varying strategies for, 122

The Change Masters (Kanter), 51

Change models. *See* Models of change

Change processes: connecting, 121; cyclical nature of, 3; as disorderly, 119; impact of current trends on, 62; insights into, iii; models compared, 57–58; as movements, v; multiple models and, 55; new curriculums on, 2–3; outcomes and, 22; relationship with culture, 107; social-cognitive models and, 46; subverting, 98; teleological model outcomes, 33; termites as metaphor, 29; understanding, 11–12

Chaos theory, evolutionary models and, 31, 32

Charisma, 69

Closed systems, biological theories and, 60

Coalition-building: change and, 94; dialectical models and, 96–97; as political change skill, 42; as political process, vii

Cognition: cognitive reorientation and, 99; sensemaking and, 47; social-cognition models and, 44

Cognitive dissonance (cognition and change), 45

Collaboration: as current trend, 61; self-assessment and, 116–117; teleological models and, 35, 89–90

Collaborative learning as force of change, 1

Collective bargaining, dialectical models and, 42, 98

Collegium: cultures as, 65–66; cybernetic model in, 110

Commitment, employee, 74

Common language. *See* Language

Community, principle of, 9

Community-service learning as force of change, 1

Conflict: as attribute of human interaction, v; dialectical models and, 41, 43; political process and, 116; as pressure for change, 94–95

Consciousness groups, cultural models and, 51

Constancy, culture of change and, 109

Constructed interaction, 100–101, 118

Contingency as social evolutionary model, 28

Continuity, 60

Continuous quality improvement. *See* TQM (total quality management)

Contradiction (cultural models), 52

Cost constraints as force of change, 1

Criticisms: cultural models, 52–53; dialectical models, 43–44; evolutionary models, 31–32; life-cycle model, 39–40; models compared, 57–58; social-cognition models, 48–49; teleological models and, 35–36

Cross-functional teams: reengineering and, 34; social-cognition models and, 103

Cultural models: assumptions, 50; benefits and criticisms, 52–53; examined, 105–109; examined through values in, 12; examples of, 50–52; future research and, 130; and institutional change, vii; irrationality, 49; metaphors in, 52; subcultures within, 2; summary, 57–58; theory of change category, iv–v; use in educational institutions, vi

Culture. *See* Organizational culture

Cybernetics: cognition and change, 45; multiple model example, 109–110; need for different models, 121–122

Cyclic nature of change, 3, 9, 20, 38

D

Dawson's processual change model, 51

Decision-making: change models and, 61; irrationality in, 108; organized anarchical, 71–72; promoting, 119–120

Definition, social-cognition models and, 103

Degree of change, iv, 16–17

Demographics as force of change, 1

Determinism, 25

Developmental culture, 65

Developmental theories: life-cycle model and, 39; studies on models, 92–93

Dialectical models: assumptions, 40–41; benefits and criticisms, 43–44; deterministic nature, 44; empowerment approaches, 42; examined, 93–98; examples of, 41–43; and influence, 96; informal processes in, 97; interest groups, 94–96; Nordvall on, 26; opposing forces, 40; social-cognition models and, 48; summary, 57–58; theory of change category, iv–v. *See also* Political models

Dichotomies (planned and adaptive change), 27

Differentiation, evolutionary models and, 81–82

Diffusion, as change strategy, 13–15

Dimensions, 12

Diversity: accreditation agencies and, 62; as current trend, 61; as force of change, 1

Double-loop learning: second-order change as, 16; social-cognition models and, 46, 99–100

Durkhiem, Emile, 125

E

Ecology, population: evolutionary models and, 31; as social evolutionary model, 28

Ecology of higher education, 62

Educational institutions: change process insights, iii; changes in curriculum, 2–3; characteristics of, 66–67, 120; as mature industry, 92; nature of higher education, v–vii, 59–77

Einstein, Albert, 25

Emotional intelligence, 37

Employee commitment, 74

Emulation: future research and, 130; social-cognition models and, 104–105

Enterprise-based authority, 69

Entrepreneurial nature: evolutionary models and, 85–86; of institutions, 66

Environmental factors: curriculum for changes, 2–3; evolutionary models and, 83–84; levels in organization, 18; types of change, v; vulnerability from environment, 126. *See also* External environment; Internal environment

Evaluation phase (diffusion model), 13

The Evolution of Educational Thought (Durkhiem), 125

Evolutionary models: adaptation in, 14; assumptions, 28–30; benefits and criticisms, 31–32; classification of change, 17–18; and competing forces, 83; dialectical models and, 43; differentiation, 81–82; examined, 80–86; examples, 30–31; external environments and, 15; focus of change and, 19; frustration with, 112; future research about, 126; homeostasis, 29; life-cycle models and, 36; need for different models, 122; Nordvall on, 26; openness, 29; prevalence in literature, 27; summary, 57–58; theory of change category, iv; use in educational institutions, vii

Experiential learning, institutionalization and, 14

Expert power, 68

External environment: balancing with internal, 118–119; current trends from, 61; evolutionary models and, 18, 31, 85; as force of change, 15; future research and, 126; openness and, 29; pressures of, 64; social-cognition models and, 49. *See also* Internal environment

F

Facilitators of change: constructed interaction as, 118; culture of risk as, 109; dialectical models as, 93; paradigm shifts, 108; in social-cognition models, 48; teleological models and, 91

Faculty: accreditation agencies and, 62; part-time and contract, 61; turnover in, 74

Feedback loops: Birnbaum and, 128; cybernetic model and, 110

First-order change: as concept, iv; homeostasis and, 29; as incremental change, 16; life-cycle models and, 38; teleological models and, 33

Focus of change, iv, 19–20

Forces of change: collaborative learning as, 1; components of, 15; as concept, iv; future research and, 126; grants and funding, 63

Future-envisioning: cultural models and, 50; social-cognition models and, 47

G

Generative change: as concept, iv; examined, 20; teleological models and, 33
Goal-setting: ambiguity in, 74–75; teleological models and, 33
Governance. *See* Shared governance
Grener model on organizational growth, 37–38
Groundwork, laying, 116–117
Growth stages in organizations, 37–38

H

Hegelian-Marxian perspective (dialectical models), 40
Hierarchy, administrative power and, 72
Higher education. *See* Educational institutions
History and tradition: cultural models and, vii, 105–106; response to world wars, 131
Homeostasis: creating, 118–119; evolutionary model key concept, 29; evolutionary models and, vii, 82
Homogenization, 104–105
Human resource lens, multidimensional thinking and, 54

I

Identification: in educational institutions, vi; as outcome, 37
Identity: connecting change process to, 121; evolutionary models and normative, 85; future research and, 129; image and success in, 76; lifecycle model and, 37, 93
Ideology: dialectical models and patriarchal, 43; models of change and, 25
Image: awareness of, 120; change models and, 61; in educational institutions, vi; future research and, 129; social-cognition models and, 103–104; and success, 75–76
Imitation: future research and, 130; social-cognition models and, 104–105
Implementation phase (institutionalization), 13
Independence: change models and, 61; of environment, 63–64
Innovation: adaptability and, 117; defined, 14
Institutional isomorphism, 99, 104–105
Institutionalization: as change strategy, 13–15; social-cognition models and, 103
Institutionalization phase (institutionalization), 13–14
Intentionality. *See* Planned change; Unplanned change
Interactivity: evolutionary model key concept, 29; of strategies, vii, 131
Interdependent organizations: change models and, 61; overview, 62–63
Interest phase (diffusion model), 13
Internal environment: balancing with external forces, 118–119; dialectical model and, 44; as force of change, 15; teleological models and, 33
Interpretation: cognition and change, 45; social-cognition models and, 103
Interpretive strategy: cultural models and, 52; solution example, 3
Irrationality, cultural models and, 49, 108

K

Kanter, Rosabeth, 51
Kellogg Foundation, 2, 63
Knowledge structures (cognition and change), 45

L

Language: change definitions, iii–iv; change process insights, iii; social-cognition models and, 102

Leadership: adaptability and, 117; change model and collective, 7; dialectical models and, 41; reengineering and, 34; social-cognition models and, 45, 47; teleological models and, 33, 89–90

Learning models: double-loop learning, 16, 46, 99–100; institutionalization and experiential, 14; life-cycle models and, 37; single-loop learning, 16, 46, 99–100; social-cognition models and, 101–102; solution example, 3

Legitimization, social-cognition models and, 103

Levels of change, 18, 93

Lewin, Kurt, 79

Life-cycle models: assumptions, 36–37; benefits and criticisms, 39–40; communication processes, 37; developmental theories, 39; dialectical model and, 44; educational institutions and, vii; examined, 92–93; future research and, 128–129; identify development and, 121; summary, 57–58; theory of change category, iv–v; as variation of evolutionary model, 26

Loosely coupled systems: adaptability and, 117; change hidden in, 125; evolutionary models and, 82; future research, 126; overview, 70–71; recommendations for, 118–119; shared governance and, 120; social-cognition models and, 99–100

M

Management: growing managerialism, 95–96, 129; life-cycle models and, 37; mapping processes as techniques, 34

Management by objectives (MBO), 88

Managerial culture, 65

Mapping processes, 34

Marxist theory, dialectical models and, 42

Measurement: lack of, vi; outcomes and, 22; of success, 76

Mediation: dialectical models and, 98; as political process, vii

Mental models: interaction and, 118; social-cognition models and, 100; templates of behavior and, 104

Metamorphosis, scale of change and, 18

Metaphors: for cultural models, 50; for dialectical models, 41; for evolutionary models, 29; for life-cycle models, 37; models compared, 57–58; for social-cognition models, 45, 102; for teleological models, 33, 91

Methodogy, future research and, 132

Mission: change and, 66–67; examination of, 3; reexamining, 1; teleological models and, 87–88

Mobilization phase (institutionalization), 13

Model compared with theory, 26

Models of change: aligning, 127; combining, v; compared, 57–58; developmental theories, 92–93; examined, 79–112; guidelines, 123; ideology and, 25; levels of change and, 131; multiple models, 53–55; need for different, 121–122; for theories of change, iv–v; typology of, vii, 26–28. *See also* individual model names

Motivators: in change decisions, 108; in cultural models, 50; dialectical models and, 41

Multiculturalism: as focus of change, 19–20; as force of change, 1

Multidimensional thinking, 16, 54
Multiple models: combining, 122–123; examined, 109–111; overview, 53–55

N

Negotiation: Bergquist's negotiating culture, 65; as political change skill, 42; as political process, vii
Networking, 42
Nonprofit sector, 60, 67

O

Observation compared with perception, 12
Open learning system (Pettigrew), 55
Open systems, biological theories and, 60
Openness (evolutionary model), 29
Opposing forces in dialectical models, 40
Organizational change: definition of, 12; future research on, 125–132; key to successful, 59–77
Organizational culture: Bergquist's four cultures, 65; change models and, 61; cultural models and, 107; examination of, 3; and impact on change, 115; principles, 9; status and, 66–67; tied with attitude, 19; uniqueness of, 65–66
Organizational development: first-order change and, 16; stages of growth, 37–38; teleological models and, 32, 33
Outcomes: assessment of, 62; change process and, 22; as concept, iv; difficulty measuring, 22; institutionalization as, 13–14; models compared, 57–58; organizational identity, 37; as target of change, 15; in teleological models, 33
Outsourcing, 73, 91

P

Paradigm shifts: cultural models and, 50, 51, 107–108; second-order change and, 17; social-cognition models and, 47
Paradigms: cognition and change, 45; teleological models and, 33
Perception compared with observation, 12
Persistence: dialectical models and, 97; employee commitment and, 74; value of, 109
Persuasion: dialectical models and, 96; as political process, vii
Pettigrew's open learning system, 55
Pew Charitable Trusts Leadership Award, 2
Phases: in diffusion model, 13; in institutionalization, 13–14
Planned change: as concept, iv; dichotomies, 27; intentionality and, 20–21; internal environment and, 15; literature focus on, 3–4; response times and, 21; as teleological model, 32. *See also* Unplanned change
Planning. *See* Strategic planning
Plasticity: cultural models and, 53; teleological models and, 36
Political lens: awareness of, 115–116; multidimensional thinking and, 54; prevalence of, 66
Political models: combining strategies, 119; concerns with, 111–112; future research and, 129; need for different models, 122; process change and, 94, 95, 115–116; use in educational institutions, vi–vii. *See also* Dialectical models

ASHE-ERIC
Higher Education Reports

The mission of the Educational Resources Information Center (ERIC) system is to improve American education by increasing and facilitating the use of educational research and information on practice in the activities of learning, teaching, educational decision making, and research, wherever and whenever these activities take place.

Since 1983, the ASHE-ERIC Higher Education Report series has been published in cooperation with the Association for the Study of Higher Education (ASHE). Starting in 2000, the series has been published by Jossey-Bass in conjunction with the ERIC Clearinghouse on Higher Education.

Each monograph is the definitive analysis of a tough higher education problem, based on thorough research of pertinent literature and institutional experiences. Topics are identified by a national survey. Noted practitioners and scholars are then commissioned to write the reports, with experts providing critical reviews of each manuscript before publication.

Six monographs in the series are published each year and are available on individual and subscription bases. To order, use the order form at the back of this issue.

Qualified persons interested in writing a monograph for the series are invited to submit a proposal to the National Advisory Board. As the preeminent literature review and issue analysis series in higher education, the Higher Education Reports are guaranteed wide dissemination and provide national exposure for accepted candidates. Execution of a monograph requires at least a minimal familiarity with the ERIC database, including *Resources in Education* and the current *Index to Journals in Education*. The objective of these reports is to bridge conventional wisdom and practical research.

Advisory Board

Susan Frost
Office of Institutional Planning and Research
Emory University

Kenneth Feldman
SUNY at Stony Brook

Anna Ortiz
Michigan State University

James Fairweather
Michigan State University

Lori White
Stanford University

Esther E. Gottlieb
West Virginia University

Carol Colbeck
Pennsylvania State University

Jeni Hart
University of Arizona

Understanding and Facilitating Organizational Change in the 21st Century

Review Panelists and
Consulting Editors

Leonard Baird
Ohio State University

Nancy Gafney
Council for Graduate Schools

Ronald Lee
University of Nebraska

Jeffrey Milem
University of Maryland

Suzanne Ortega
University of Nebraska

Anne S. Pruitt-Logan
Council of Graduate Schools

John C. Smart
University of Memphis

Recent Titles

Volume 28 ASHE-ERIC Higher Education Reports

1. The Changing Nature of the Academic Deanship
   Mimi Wolverton, Walter H. Gmelch, Joni Montez, and Charles T. Nies

2. Faculty Compensation Systems: Impact on the Quality of Higher Education
   Terry P. Sutton, Peter J. Bergerson

3. Socialization of Graduate and Professional Students in Higher Education:
   A Perilous Passage?
   John C. Weidman, Darla J. Twale, Elizabeth Leahy Stein

Volume 27 ASHE-ERIC Higher Education Reports

1. The Art and Science of Classroom Assessment: The Missing Part of Pedagogy
   Susan M. Brookhart

2. Due Process and Higher Education: A Systemic Approach to Fair Decision Making
   Ed Stevens

3. Grading Students' Classroom Writing: Issues and Strategies
   Bruce W. Speck

4. Posttenure Faculty Development: Building a System for Faculty Improvement
   and Appreciation
   Jeffrey W. Alstete

5. Digital Dilemma: Issues of Access, Cost, and Quality in Media-Enhanced and Distance
   Education
   Gerald C. Van Dusen

6. Women and Minority Faculty in the Academic Workplace: Recruitment, Retention, and
   Academic Culture
   Adalberto Aguirre, Jr.

7. Higher Education Outside of the Academy
   Jeffrey A. Cantor

8. Academic Departments: How They Work, How They Change
   *Barbara E. Walvoord, Anna K. Carey, Hoke L. Smith, Suzanne W. Soled,
   Philip K. Way, Debbie Zorn*

Understanding and Facilitating Organizational Change in the 21st Century

Volume 26 ASHE-ERIC Higher Education Reports

Volume 25 ASHE-ERIC Higher Education Reports

Volume 24 ASHE-ERIC Higher Education Reports

Volume 23 ASHE-ERIC Higher Education Reports

Back Issue/Subscription Order Form

Copy or detach and send to:
Jossey-Bass, 989 Market Street, San Francisco, CA 94103-1741

Call or fax toll free!
Phone 888-378-2537 6AM-5PM PST; Fax 800-605-2665

Individual reports:	Please send me the following reports at $24 each
	(Important: please include series initials and issue number, such as AEHE 27:1)

1. AEHE _____

_____

_____

$ _____ Total for individual reports

$ _____ Shipping charges (for individual reports *only;* subscriptions are exempt from shipping charges): Up to $30, add $5^{50} • $30^{01}–$50, add $6^{50} $50^{01}–$75, add $8 • $75^{01}–$100, add $10 • $100^{01}–$150, add $12 Over $150, call for shipping charge

Subscriptions   Please ❑ start my subscription to *ASHE-ERIC Higher Education Reports* at the following rate (6 issues):
U.S.: $108   Canada: $188   All others: $256

$ _____ Total individual reports and subscriptions (Add appropriate sales tax for your state for individual reports. No sales tax on U.S. subscriptions. Canadian residents, add GST for subscriptions and individual reports.)

Federal Tax ID 135593032   GST 89102-8052

❑ Payment enclosed (U.S. check or money order only)

❑ VISA, MC, AmEx, Discover Card # _____ Exp. date _____

Signature _____ Day phone _____

❑ Bill me (U.S. institutional orders only. Purchase order required.)

Purchase order #_____

Name _____

Address _____

_____

Phone_____ E-mail _____

For more information about Jossey-Bass, visit our Web site at:
www.josseybass.com   **PRIORITY CODE = ND1**

Dr. Adrianna Kezar is assistant professor at the University of Maryland, College Park; editor of the ASHE-ERIC Higher Education Report Series and faculty director for the Institute for Emerging Women Leaders in Higher Education.

Before her appointment with the University of Maryland, Kezar was a faculty member at George Washington University and director of the ERIC Clearinghouse on Higher Education. As director of the ERIC Clearinghouse, her main responsibilities included developing research and communicating in a meaningful way to higher education professionals. Prior appointments also include administrative associate for the Vice President for Student Affairs and coordinator for the Center for Research on Learning and Teaching, both at the University of Michigan, Ann Arbor.

Kezar has served on editorial boards for *The Review of Higher Education, Blacks in Education,* and the *Journal of Higher Education.* She is a elected Board member of the American Association for Higher Education, AERA-Division J Council, and Association for the Study of Higher Education Publication Committee, Association of American Colleges and Universities' Peer Review and Knowledge Network, National TRIO Clearinghouse, and the American Council on Education's CIRP Research Cooperative.

Kezar holds a Ph.D. and an M.A. in higher education administration from the University of Michigan, and a B.A. from the University of California, Los Angeles. Her research focuses on higher education leadership, diversity issues, organizational theory, systems change, and administration. Her work has been published in many journals, including *The Journal of Higher Education, The Review of Higher Education, Research in Higher Education, AAHE Bulletin, Community College Review, New Directions in Higher Education, New Directions in Institutional Research, About Campus,* and *The ERIC Review.* Her most recent publications include: *Beyond the Gap Between Research and Practice,* 2000; and *Reconceptualizing the Collegiate Ideal: The Current State and Future Prospects of the Idea of Campus* (1999, Jossey-Bass). Her research has been used to guide the development of a national leadership institute for female administrators in higher education.

CPSIA information can be obtained at www.ICGtesting.com
Printed in the USA
LVOW06s2202151213

365463LV00003B/259/A

9 780787 958374